"Competition in the corporate world has never been as fierce. Quantum Business offers an innovative strategy for business people to capitalize on personal strengths to maximize performance and succeed in today's business environment."
– Patrick Foley, Chairman and CEO
DHL Worldwide Express

"This is a great book about learning and growing—from theory to everyday actions. Bobbi is a great and enthusiastic teacher and trainer. Read this book! It will give you the tools to keep learning and succeeding long into the future."
– Larry Wilson, Founder
Pecos River Learning
Co-author, *The One Minute Salesperson*

"The rock solid foundation of the Eight Keys of Excellence, upon which Quantum Business is based, provides a framework that learners of all ages should incorporate into their personal life long self-development journey."
– Ned Herrmann
Author, *The Creative Brain*

"If every business were run on the principles described in Quantum Business, not only would they be more successful but the world would be a better place."
– Joyce Wycoff, Executive Director
Innovation Network
Author, *Transformation Thinking*

"Great book for new organizations to incorporate into their culture and for existing organizations that ought to change."
– R. Dale Scott, President
Glacier Park Inc.

Also by Bobbi DePorter with Mike Hernacki
QUANTUM LEARNING: Unleashing the Genius in You

QUANTUM
BUSINESS

Achieving Success Through
Quantum Learning

by

Bobbi DePorter

with Mike Hernacki

A Dell Trade Paperback

A DELL TRADE PAPERBACK

Published by
Dell Publishing
a division of
Bantam Doubleday Dell Publishing Group, Inc.
1540 Broadway
New York, New York 10036

Designed by Linus Saint James
Illustrations by Ellen Duris

Library of Congress Cataloging in Publication Data
DePorter, Bobbi.
    Quantum Business: achieving success through quantum learning/
Bobbi DePorter with Mike Hernacki
    p.   cm.
    Includes index.
    ISBN: 0-440-50741-3
    1. Organizational learning.   2. Active learning.   3. Success in business.   I. Hernacki, Mike.   II. Title.
    HD58.82.D47   1997
    650.1--dc20   96-30374
                                                                          CIP

Printed in the United States of America
Published simultaneously in Canada
May 1997
10 9 8 7 6 5 4 3 2 1
Permissions appear on page 361.

I dedicate this book

to Joe, for his loving support
and partnership in Learning Forum,

and in memory of my father and mother
who guided me with great wisdom and love.

— B.D.

Contents

Acknowledgments

The principles in this book started at Hawthorne/Stone, a real estate and investment firm that was anything but ordinary. I thank the original partners there, Marshall Thurber, Rob Cassil, and Bill Raymond for tremendous learning and growth. My learning continued in quantum leaps during my partnership with Marshall in the Burklyn Business School. Marshall is a masterful teacher, able to take complex theory and create powerful and creative workshops that have changed the lives of many, including myself. I thank my co-founders of SuperCamp, Greg Simmons for the launch of what became Learning Forum, and Eric Jensen for his enormous contribution and ongoing support.

This book was an amazing team effort. I am most appreciative to Mike Hernacki who was instrumental in the creation of the book, giving ongoing guidance, direction, and writing expertise; to Shelby Reeder for her writing support; to Linus Saint James for his graphic design; to Vicki T. Gibbs for her review and input; and Ellen Duris for her illustrations. All of us worked together in a creative, synergistic atmosphere to create this book and I give a very special thank you to the team!

The Learning Forum staff have continuously supported this book. In particular I thank my husband and partner, Joe Chapon, and again, Shelby Reeder and

Linus Saint James. In addition I thank Lori Walker, Renee Switzer, Mark Ogle, Beth Talmon, Rob Dunton, and Tricia Huppert for their support and contribution. I thank Mark Reardon for his talent and insights while at Learning Forum and for his creative influence on and facilitation of our programs.

Many people's ideas and methods helped form the concepts in this book. I especially thank Grant DePorter for his enthusiasm and skill in using memory techniques and for co-writing the memory chapters with me; Steve Snyder for his reading methods and stories; John LeTellier, Susan Dellinger, Dawna Markova, and Barbara Given for their concepts of "learning styles"; Tony Buzan and Vanda North for their review and Mind Maps; and Nancy Margulies for her Mindscapes.

I also thank—for insights, content, and general support—Linda Brown-Schaeff, Steve Curtis, Joyce Wycoff, Robert Kiyosaki, D.C. Harrison, Blair Singer, Carol Maero, and David Neenan—and my family, Grant and Joanna DePorter, Dana and Michael Harvey, and Don DePorter.

I am most appreciative for the guidance I received from my literary agent, Sandra Dijkstra; my publicist, Andrea Nordstrom Caughey; and my editor at Dell, Stephanie Gunning, in making this book a reality.

— B.D.

QUANTUM
BUSINESS

1

From Real Life to Business School and Back

 What business philosophies are most likely to lead you to personal/ professional success?

 How do attitude and environment affect results?

 What are some benefits of creating a "win/win" situation?

Note: Every chapter in this book begins with a list of questions and ends with a list of answers. This is to help you anticipate what you will learn, and then review what you have learned. It's a valuable technique to use whenever you're reading for information.

QUANTUM BUSINESS

The workplace is changing dramatically right before your eyes. With costs escalating and profits being squeezed, companies are "downsizing," which usually means asking fewer people to produce the same amount of work. Maybe you or someone you know has been "downsized" out of a job. Maybe you've been forced into a completely different job in order to preserve your career. Even if you weren't forced to, you may have switched fields because you found that the one you trained for doesn't offer the opportunities you want. Switching fields is more common than ever before. As the millennium approaches, we find that most college graduates in the U.S. are working in jobs outside the fields in which they hold their degrees. In fact, according to the U.S. Department of Education (National Center for Education Statistics, August, 1993), only 39 percent of 1990 college graduates were working in a job related to their field of study just one year after graduation. As the years go on, the percentage drops so that in a few more years only a tiny percentage actually do the job they studied for.

If you're an employer, you may have experienced the agony of having to let people go when business is slow. This is especially upsetting if the people are good workers, but have not upgraded their knowledge and skills to keep pace with changes in your industry.

Today, technology is changing so rapidly and companies are trying so desperately to remain profitable that everyone is being challenged to learn, and learn fast. Employees are facing unprecedented changes in job descriptions and employer expectations. Learning a completely new job—or even keeping up with developments in your old job—can be frightening. But how much choice do you have? Whereas once workers were

Captain "Q" shows you how Quantum Business methods help you keep pace with today's changing workplace.

Captain "Q" is a character we created to help you visualize the concepts in this book. He's a superhero with a superbrain — just like yours.

receiving benefits such as flexible hours, part-time work, and the freedom to telecommute, now thousands of people are seeing their positions "reengineered" out of existence. As a result, most people are grateful just to have a job.

While the pace of change is taking its toll on businesses of all sizes, a small business is particularly vulnerable if it doesn't have the ability to adapt. Entrepreneurs must constantly learn new systems and technologies to stay profitable and make their businesses more competitive. If you're in business for yourself, you may find yourself falling behind, despite your best efforts.

Going through tremendous changes can leave you feeling lost, lonely, and powerless. But you do have power—more than you may realize. It is inside you right now, the potential to take control of your life, to jump-start your career, or move your business ahead. The key to this power is learning—and by learning, I don't mean just learning to read and write. The spectrum of learning covers far more than academic subjects and skills. We all must learn how to think, interact with others, manage our work, and our lives.

Learning isn't only something you do in school, or in seminars. Learning is something you do all day, every day. It includes the foundation and principles upon which you build your life. It includes the environment in which you spend your days and nights. To say that learning is the key to a successful life is like saying that legs are the key to successful walking. I cannot conceive of a life of growth, progress, and accomplishment without the constant learning that makes these things happen.

The Amazing Human Learning Machine

We are all born with an insatiable desire to learn, and a remarkable ability to do so. Unfortunately, most of us lose

Learning is composed of many elements . . .

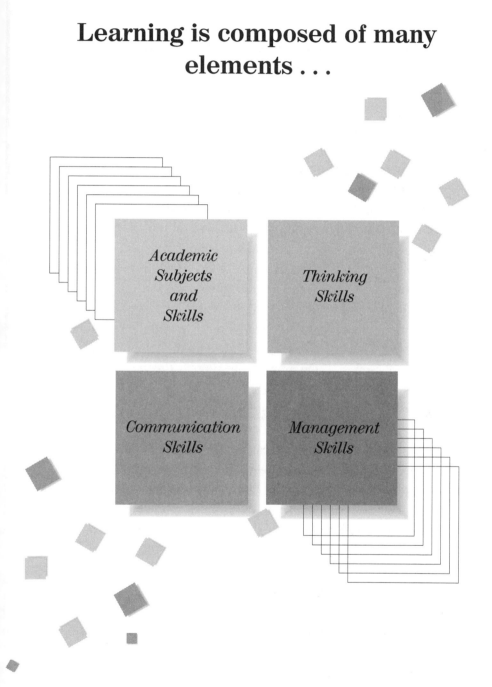

Academic Subjects and Skills

Thinking Skills

Communication Skills

Management Skills

our enthusiasm sometime during our school years. Once we leave school, we consider our learning days to be over. Then, when we're required to purposely learn something new, we resist and become angry or frustrated. In the rapidly changing world of business, this attitude will almost certainly sabotage professional success.

To prevent this from happening, you need to return to that time in your life when learning was an unquenchable thirst. You need to make learning fun again. If you can do that, plus pick up some important skills that help you in other areas of your life, you'll be well along the path to achieving your personal and professional goals.

Quantum Business is based on the premise that learning can, and should, be fun. It's a follow-up to a book I wrote several years ago called *Quantum Learning.* The first book was written for anyone who needs to learn anything. This one is more specific: it applies the principles and techniques of Quantum Learning to the unique challenges you face in the world of work.

But it takes more than a set of learning skills to achieve the balanced success that makes life enjoyable. It also takes the right attitude and a healthy environment. Woven throughout this book are the "8 Keys to Excellence," guidelines for developing a successful attitude and creating a positive environment. This synthesis of environment, attitude, and skills unleashes your power to create a more effective, confident, and successful business and personal life.

The story of Quantum Learning is closely linked to my own story and the path I followed from housewife to millionaire to entrepreneur. Along the way, Quantum Learning grew into a comprehensive approach promoting both personal development and business success. It has

With the right attitude and healthy environment, the human learning machine can accomplish great feats.

been used by adults in the workplace and students at every level from elementary school to doctorate with phenomenal results. The results have been phenomenal for the thousands who have used it.

The "Miracle" of Hawthorne/Stone

In 1974, I was a housewife in San Francisco, staying at home and raising my two children. Though I loved my kids and enjoyed my role, I found myself starting to feel anxious and depressed. I yearned to do something for myself, to feel a sense of personal and professional achievement. I was pretty sure I wanted to get involved in business, but wasn't at all sure what form that involvement might take. Each day I would scan the want ads, hoping something would pop out at me. Sure enough, one morning I was drawn to an intriguing ad for a salesperson in a real estate firm, promising lots of money and personal growth. I called and set up an interview.

The firm was Hawthorne/Stone, one of the most successful real estate ventures in San Francisco. I took the job, and was soon introduced to a set of principles that are so valuable, and work so well, they've stayed with me for more than 20 years. These principles have literally been the foundation for everything I've done in my career, including the incredibly successful approach to learning that's the subject of this book.

Hawthorne/Stone's unique way of doing business enabled many people to achieve a level of success they had previously only dreamed about. The key to this success was an office environment like none of us had ever experienced before. The firm's founders, Marshall Thurber, Rob Cassil, and Bill Raymond, cultivated an open, supportive workplace in which the focus was on relationships, not on procedures or office politics. At our regular staff meetings, we were encouraged to share our experiences—both business and personal—with everyone in the firm. This gave each of us a feeling of belonging and of being supported. The meetings stressed goals and achievements, and we began each session by sharing positive things that had happened to us. The environment was safe and accepting, never negative or critical. This encouraged all of us to be creative in our thinking and courageous in our actions.

Hawthorne/Stone actively promoted a win/win philosophy long before "win/win" became a popular buzzword. If the firm and the people we were dealing with couldn't all win, we'd abandon the project. The founding partners also realized that while the salespeople in the office had the opportunity to make large sums of money (six of them earned over $200,000 apiece in their second year), the administrative staff's salary was fixed. This inequity was a divisive factor, undermining the harmony so critical to the firm's success. As an incentive to get everyone pulling in the same direction, the partners developed a bonus system. Salaried employees received a 10 percent increase in their pay for every $100,000 the agency earned above its annual goal. One year, the lowest paid employee earned over $40,000.

Generally, the firm's goal was economic independence for everyone. But it was clear that we'd never let that come about at the expense of the company's values. The partners repeatedly told us they wanted the business to "come from the point of view of total responsibility, of serving, of being totally honest, and of doing the job in a way that is fun and supportive." This wasn't just talk; it was the way we did business every day.

Reduced to a series of one-sentence statements, the

corporate philosophy was:

- Be honest in communicating.
- Speak with Good Purpose.
- Keep agreements.
- Be willing to share and support so everyone succeeds.
- Take responsibility for creating an abundant environment.
- Drop what isn't working.
- Acknowledge the achievements of others.

These statements became the basis of our 8 Keys of Excellence (see Chapter 2), which are the guiding principles of my company, Learning Forum. I've woven the 8 Keys into the fabric of this book because I believe you cannot learn, grow, and develop in business just by learning techniques. Your thoughts and actions must be grounded in a solid philosophy that seeks to benefit you and everyone you deal with in business.

At Hawthorne/Stone, clear, honest communication helped ease the stress while it enabled us to feel closer and more trusting of one another. To "Speak with Good Purpose" meant eliminating gossip, profanity, and negative or defeating statements. This in turn helped create a positive atmosphere. Keeping agreements showed integrity and respect for others. In a hectic and highly specialized business, we all needed to know we could count on one another to follow through on our commitments.

We were also willing to share the wealth as well as the work, and to support one another's journey to success. Unlike many real estate offices, ours was a noncompetitive workplace. Though every agent wanted to be the one to make the sale, we openly discussed our work, took calls for one another, and shared information. We celebrated one another's achievements; when one person won, the whole organization won. We believed we were responsible for what we created, so we worked hard to create an abundant environment. We were rich both financially and emotionally.

We also agreed to let go of whatever didn't work. There was no hanging on, feeling sorry, or hoping a negative would magically change into a positive. When something didn't work, we refused to take it personally. We dropped it and moved on to more productive efforts. Most important, we acted out of the belief that the more we gave, the more we would receive. Supporting and caring for one another and our clients proved to be a much more successful approach than the stereotypical "dog-eat-dog" business philosophy. We were excited and motivated about what we were doing and we were creating a working model of what we considered the ideal business environment.

Yes, this philosophy was unorthodox, but it got results. Many of the salespeople were generating high six-figure incomes (close to a million dollars a year). By some estimates we had higher per capita earnings than any other company in America at the time.

But our success was more than just financial. People were being given the opportunity to develop personally as well. A member of our sales staff once said, "I've gone from self-consciousness to self-confidence. I used to think everybody was guarding who they were and what they had and wouldn't give me anything; consequently, I had to guard 'me' in business dealings . . . I used to feel that in order to get, I had to take from people. Now I can give—and the more I give, the more I get. It's a lot more pleasant this way."

When I started, the partners made it clear to me that in order to keep working there, I would have to make at least

$30,000 a year. At the time, with my limited business experience, that seemed an unreachable goal. I'd never made anywhere near that amount of money before. To my surprise, my first day on the job I made a deal worth a little over $30,000 to me! Within a few years I had acquired a net worth of over a million dollars and been named a junior partner in the firm.

As you might expect, our success and business practices attracted a lot of attention. Everyone we talked to wanted to know more about what we were doing and why we were so successful. They wanted to learn how to replicate the results we were achieving. Marshall Thurber and I were eager to share this information. It seemed that a natural next step would be to open our own business school. So that's exactly what we did.

A New Breed of Business School

Full of optimism and convinced of the value of what we had to teach, Marshall and I opened the Burklyn Business School in 1978 in rural Vermont. The campus was an historic landmark named Burklyn Hall. It included a country estate and mansion, an inn, a restaurant, stables, and an indoor riding arena. All of this was nestled on 600 acres of green rolling hills. The relaxed, serene setting felt more like a resort than a school.

The curriculum combined traditional business subjects with learning skills, underpinned by the Hawthorne/Stone philosophy. Courses were taught holistically, based on our conviction that students needed to understand all aspects of business, not just one area. We decided to produce generalists armed with the knowledge to develop their own businesses rather than specialists able to manage only one part of a company. We also treated the students holistically—that is, viewing them as a whole person rather than just a learner. We offered a steady diet of exercise classes, meditation, and personal development workshops.

Terry Allen, a university professor who taught at Burklyn, said, "Using these innovative methods, we were able to teach two years' worth of material in six weeks." In case studies Terry developed for the Harvard Business School, he had never seen anything like it.

Many of our students already held a business degree and were managers or business owners. Others wanted to build their own businesses, but didn't know where to begin. The instructors were entrepreneurs, psychologists, and business philosophers—all at the top of their fields. Our staff included accountants, marketing experts, and guest lecturers such as Pete Wanger, founder of Granny Goose potato chips; Porter Briggs, publisher and former White House Fellow; and the late Buckminster Fuller, architect, inventor, and one of the greatest minds of the twentieth century.

Our teaching methods were experimental and constantly evolving. We never assumed that we knew the best way to teach something, or that we couldn't learn from the students as much as they learned from us. In fact, the students participated actively in the development of our methods. Eager to learn faster and more efficiently, they willingly tried new learning techniques.

One time the students were grumbling that their instructor was relying too heavily on traditional teaching methods. In most academic circles this was equivalent to mutiny. Marshall brought the class to a halt, confronted the teacher, and demanded that he try something else. The result was a series of support groups, a system that eventually was adopted throughout the school. Six to 10 students would meet with their instructors before class, review the curriculum, and offer suggestions on how to make the course more meaningful and participatory. Students were also encouraged to critique the instructors in writing. Soon it became commonplace for students to work with the instructors in redesigning the courses.

The learning methods we used were based on the work of the legendary Bulgarian educator, Dr. Georgi Lozanov. His methods are collectively referred to as "accelerative learning," and include techniques such as creating a supportive, positive, and stress-free environment; putting students in a relaxed state so they'll be more receptive to learning; using baroque music to create mood and state; and varying tone and intonation while speaking. At Burklyn, we also used hands-on participatory methods, plus visuals and music. This type of teaching engages both sides of the brain, and has been scientifically proven to greatly increase learning speed and comprehension.

One of the most revolutionary examples of this method is "The Accounting Game™," a process that teaches the basics of accounting conceptually. Unlike traditional accounting courses, the emphasis is not on numbers, but on account-ability. In the initial exercises, students use pieces of colored paper and very simple numbers to learn how to keep the books for a child's sidewalk lemonade stand. Mercedes Merrill-Wilson, a professional accountant who took our course, said it gave her a "better understanding of what accounting is all about than four years of college ever did."

The Accounting Game continues to be taught today by Educational Discoveries, Inc., to corporations, including Kodak, Kellogg Company, and Caterpillar; and in public seminars. Because of its unique application of the teaching

The Burklyn Business School was based on a unique approach to understanding business.

Traditional Business School	Burklyn Business School
▪▪ Training managers	▪▪ Training entrepreneurs
▪▪ Developing specialists	▪▪ Developing generalists
▪▪ Use established teaching methods	▪▪ Use experimental teaching methods
▪▪ Only teach students	▪▪ Teach and learn from students
▪▪ Instructors are full-time teachers	▪▪ Instructors were business professionals

of accounting and finances, the Accounting Game was granted a U.S. patent.

I believe the key to Burklyn's success was the high level of safety and trust. Students were able to spend hours one-on-one with instructors, receiving valuable advice on their future business projects. The instructors also felt it was a learning experience for them. "One day I found myself critiquing this unsound business project," said instructor Dick Gunter, "but I was doing it in a tender, reinforcing way. I couldn't believe my ears. This just wasn't my style. I'm sure that what opened me up to this sort of approach—it certainly wasn't a conscious effort—was the incredibly supportive atmosphere at Burklyn."

Burklyn surpassed even our most optimistic expectations. While traditional business schools were turning out managers, our graduates became entrepreneurs with not only the know-how, but also the self-confidence to succeed. Terry Allen told us, "On an experiential level, the students learn a set of principles that you won't find in textbooks distributed in most graduate schools of business. I'm talking about the 'win/win' philosophy that hallmarks Hawthorne/Stone, the highest possible ethical standards, the support of everyone in the organization, and the insistence that management be aligned in terms of the organization's goals."

Students also discovered that school could be fun. At Burklyn, learning was an exciting, meaningful, joyful process, and even those who had disliked school their whole lives wound up enjoying it in spite of themselves.

Disaster Strikes

A few years after establishing Burklyn, Marshall and I saw our dream school come to what we thought was an untimely end. One of our professors showed us a system that he had developed for making money in stock options. We monitored it for weeks and were excited to see it actually got the results he promised. We eagerly began investing money—not just our own, but that of others as well. So sure were we that the system was foolproof, we personally guaranteed the investors that they would not lose. For a while, the system turned in good profits. Eventually, however, we had so many investors and controlled so many contracts that we ourselves began affecting the market's trends. The system did not provide for this possibility and one day the market turned against us, causing all our positions to collapse completely. We lost millions of dollars in a matter of days.

Because we had guaranteed our investors that they would not lose, we had to personally cover the losses. I lost everything. All my money, my house, everything. All I had left in the world was my car, which somehow the lawyers had overlooked. But even by liquidating virtually all of my assets, I could not cover a hundred percent of the losses. So I had to personally call the investors and tell them their money was gone. This was so painful, I remember curling up in the fetal position on the floor between phone calls, trying to muster the courage to make the next call. It was a horrible experience. It seemed to me that everyone was against me, everyone hated me. But, ultimately, I realized that this too had been a learning experience, and in the end, it made me stronger. Some of the worst things I could have possibly imagined actually happened to me, and I survived.

Today, thanks to all my experiences, I understand both sides of business. I know that business involves taking risks as well as reaping rewards. Marshall and I were naive players in a field that was out of our area of expertise. We had no business speculating in the market, but we justified it by telling ourselves it was okay since all the money we were making was going to support the good work we were doing at Burklyn.

That whole experience, terrible as it was at the time, actually reinforced for me the principles we taught at Burklyn. I still believed in those concepts and so did the students. In spite of our losses, a new partnership was formed and the school continued for five more years.

Sharing the Lessons of Burklyn with Our Children

At Burklyn, many of our students were parents. When they experienced the tremendous shift in their feelings about themselves as learners and what they could accomplish, they wanted a similar experience for their own children. My two children were teenagers at the time and it seemed to me that they could benefit from a program that focused on accelerative learning. I teamed up with Eric Jensen and Greg Simmons and we started a ten-day summer learning experience for teenagers, called SuperCamp. It has been quite successful, and is still the hallmark program of Learning Forum, which I now run with my husband, Joe Chapon.

SuperCamp is patterned after Burklyn, and has a similar philosophy: We create a supportive, nurturing, win/win environment where teens experience success and build confidence in their abilities. The business curriculum has been replaced by learning-to-learn skills that can be applied to any material. We also teach communication and relationship-building techniques to help teens get along better with parents, teachers, and peers during what can be a very confusing and turbulent time of life.

Business is a two-way street requiring taking risks in order to reap rewards.

Although at the beginning it was just the three of us and we had very little capital, my partners and I were driven by our excitement and our commitment to the program. We saw what Burklyn had done for adults, and we believed our children deserved a similar opportunity to learn and grow.

In designing the program, we surveyed parents to find out what their kids needed most. While the parents were concerned about academic achievement and an ability to "make it" in life, they admitted that many of their kids suffered from low self-esteem and were uninterested in school. To raise their grades, the teens needed a boost in self-esteem as much as or more than they needed learning skills. We decided unanimously that SuperCamp would be designed to boost both self-esteem and skills.

We debuted our first program in the summer of 1982. Sixty-four dubious, mostly reluctant students showed up. Through a letter-writing campaign, we rounded up students that included children of friends, relatives, and Burklyn graduates, as well as my own two teens. Employing the same values and learning strategies used at Burklyn, we achieved fantastic results. Students significantly raised grades, became more active in schools and communities, and felt measurably better about themselves.

A Quantum Leap

Over the years, we've come to call our approach "Quantum Learning," and expanded the curriculum. Quantum Learning now encompasses a variety of methods and philosophies, but much still harks back to the days of Hawthorne/Stone. And we still emphasize three areas that were central to the Burklyn program: learning environment, mental attitude, and skills.

SuperCamp is a supportive and nurturing environment where teens experience success and build confidence.

Learning Environment

We create a safe, open, loving atmosphere where students feel free to express themselves and explore opportunities without pressure from parents or peers. Our staff is expert at creating rapport with teens, offering friendship, and modeling confidence and caring. During classes, baroque music often plays softly in the background, since Dr. Lozanov found that baroque music, with its 60 to 80 beats per minute, melodic chord structures, and instrumentation, most closely matches the body's own rhythms. Lozanov's studies showed that the music helps students to be alert yet relaxed, making them more receptive to learning. During breaks, we use upbeat popular music to stimulate play and movement. The room is decorated with affirmative, motivational signs saying things like "I am an excellent learner!" "For things to change, I must change," and "Everything I want is a belief away." We keep the room neat, cheerful, well lit, and well ventilated to preserve a "high-consciousness" atmosphere.

Mental Attitude

To achieve success, you must build a positive attitude, increase your belief in yourself, and be open to trying new things. Neuro-linguistic programming (NLP), the study of how the brain organizes information, plays a key part here. NLP explores the relationship between language and behavior. We use it to create rapport between students and teachers. Using their knowledge of NLP, our teachers avoid negative phrases, give feedback carefully and positively, and focus on solutions rather than problems.

One of the key ingredients of Quantum Learning is getting students to transform negative pictures of themselves into positive ones, first by becoming aware of negative thoughts and language, and then by adopting more positive thinking patterns. At SuperCamp we use a ropes course—physical challenges to help students build confidence by helping them break through perceived limitations.

Skills

The academic skills we teach are note-taking, reading, creativity/problem-solving, memory, and writing. Students also discover their own personal learning style and strategies for learning. Our life skills include communication and relationship-building methods. As at Burklyn, we take a whole-brain approach to teaching these skills, with the result that students absorb information more quickly and efficiently. We use games, activities, music, and action to make learning fun, as well as to increase motivation and competence. As you read this book, you'll learn more about these skills and how to apply them to your work every day.

SuperCamp has improved the lives of thousands of students. Dr. Jeannette Vos-Groenendal analyzed seven years of research using quantitative and qualitative data on over 6,000 SuperCamp graduates. She found 73% raised their grades, 84% increased self-esteem, and 98% continued to use their new skills years later.

Today, over 20,000 students have attended SuperCamp. Programs are held across the U.S. and throughout the world on prominent academic campuses. We have 18 full-time employees and over 300 summer staff. We continue to expand our programs, and have recently developed Quantum Learning teacher training seminars and school in-service programs to bring our techniques to the mainstream school systems.

Quantum Learning and You

Quantum Learning is a combination of philosophy and

strategies. It works for people of all ages. It applies in many environments: the classroom, the home, and the business world. Our company is a reflection of the Quantum Learning training programs and is run on the same foundation that was so important to the remarkable results at Hawthorne/Stone.

Good relationships and supportive environment are keys to our success. We continue to hold daily meetings to communicate, share new ideas and support one another, and to generally stay aligned. When we reach milestones in program enrollments, we celebrate with office parties and other rewarding activities. Each year, we hold a "Vision Meeting," a day dedicated to aligning our goals for the coming year, getting to know each other better and playing together. We stress responsibility and teamwork. We share the responsibility of daily tasks such as answering the phones, opening mail, and running meetings. The whole office pitches in to complete a pressing project, regardless of what department we each belong to or what position we hold. We share a willingness to trust and support one another.

Just as Burklyn graduates, who profited from the principles developed at Hawthorne/Stone, once requested a program for their children, I now receive requests from the parents of SuperCamp graduates for a program for adults. They've seen what Quantum Learning has done for their children, and they want to learn to apply those same techniques and principles in their own lives and careers—their computer companies, law offices, and yes, their real estate agencies. Thus the saga has come full circle.

This book is for those parents, and for anyone who wants to reach new levels of success. It builds on lessons from Hawthorne/Stone and Burklyn, as well as from

Quantum Learning is a body of learning methods and philosophies proven effective for all ages.

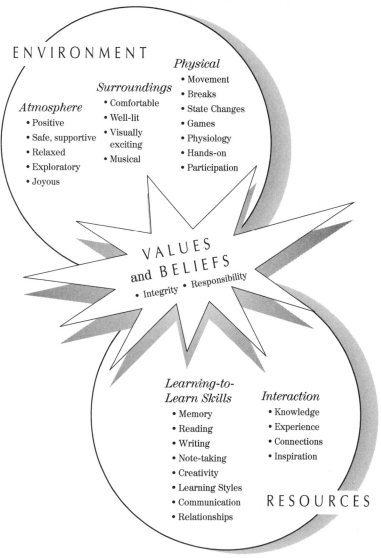

SuperCamp, and it brings these lessons back where you spend most of your waking hours: the real world of business.

Celebrate Your Learning!

! *What business philosophies are most likely to lead you to personal/professional success?*
- Be honest in communicating.
- Speak with Good Purpose.
- Keep agreements.
- Be willing to share and support so everyone succeeds.
- Take responsibility for creating an abundant environment.
- Drop what isn't working.
- Acknowledge the achievements of others.

! *How do attitude and environment affect results?*
A positive attitude and a supportive environment unleash your innate power to build a more effective, confident, creative, and successful business and personal life.

! *What are some benefits of creating a "win/win" situation?*
- Stronger team unity.
- Abundant environment.
- Customers who feel satisfied and enriched.

2

Everything Speaks:
The Impact of
Your Environment

 How does your physical space affect how you learn?

 How can careful planning help produce a more productive work environment?

 What can you do to transform meetings from boring to exciting, from wasteful to productive?

 What is the role of "vision" in your organization's future?

W hen Dr. Lozanov spoke about the influence our environment has over us, he proclaimed, "Everything speaks!" During his years of research on the power of suggestion, Lozanov found that our physical and emotional environments can greatly impact the quality of our work and lives. Based on that, he developed a teaching method known as "suggestology." (This is his term. The term "accelerative learning" was coined by his followers and includes work done by others as well as Lozanov.)

Suggestology means everything makes a suggestion. Lozanov found that a carefully controlled environment, including comfortable seating, soft lights, classical or baroque music, appropriate use of color, uplifting artwork, and inspirational messages, actually helps students learn faster and retain more information. The environment makes students feel relaxed and at ease—and as he discovered and eventually proved, the relaxed student is more receptive to learning.

This relaxed condition is called an "alpha state," wherein brain waves and heart rate slow down. When students are brought into this state they are able to physically relax, yet keep an alert mind. Lozanov also reinforced his students' attitudes with positive affirmations about themselves as learners, thereby building an atmosphere of safety and trust. Carefully measuring his results, he found that students in the alpha state learned at a much faster rate than other students and were able to remember the information for longer periods of time. Based on this, he concluded that an orchestrated environment can inspire success by telling the student's subconscious, "You can do it!"

At Learning Forum, we've adapted many of Lozanov's

teaching methods to the working world. We practice them
in our SuperCamp program and in our own organization as
well. We've repeatedly found that the seemingly insignifi-
cant details of the work environment and our interactions
with others really do make a difference. Minutiae like color,
background music, and seating arrangements can influence the tone, and thus the outcome, of a meeting. They
may also "speak" of our successes.

Details Make the Difference

To apply Quantum Learning to the business setting
requires a carefully orchestrated synthesis of the physical
and emotional environments. By physical environment, I
mean furnishings, lighting, color, music—and the atmosphere these create. "Emotional environment" includes the
choice of words used in communications, the personal relationships among the employees, the employees' internal
emotional states, and the prevailing emotions in the workplace. By carefully planning and creating our environments, we build an atmosphere of safety and trust that
Lozanov found not only helps people to learn better, but
also encourages them to participate.

A good example of how environment affects us is a
training seminar we do for summer staff called "Spirit of
SuperCamp." Much thought and planning goes into
creating an inspiring, exciting atmosphere that will pump
up energy levels and inspire teamwork. At one such
seminar, when the staff arrived for the three-day event,
they were struck by the excitement generated by the
bright colors and lively music. Hand-painted banners of
our 8 Keys of Excellence hung from the ceiling, and
posters, balloons, plants, and flowers filled the meeting
room. The theme for this particular event was "Integrity,"

one of our 8 Keys. The front of the room was dominated by a stack of nine three-foot blocks, each with one letter of the word Integrity painted on it. We decorated the participants' sleeping quarters with personalized welcome signs, and each of them received a tiny wooden block painted to signify a building block of success—a block they would take home to remind them what they experienced. Our staff put a lot of effort into making every detail "speak."

One participant said, "After being immersed in this whole environment, I felt reenergized and ready to go!"

In discussions afterward, we agreed this was one of our most successful training sessions because it created a strong bond of understanding among the employees and generated enthusiasm for upcoming programs. Every detail of the seminar supported our desired outcome and made an impact.

At our corporate office we make a similar effort. We hold an annual Office Beautification Day to clean, rearrange, replenish, and renew our work space. Each person takes responsibility for his or her own area, and shared work spaces are a group effort. The air ripples with excitement as we discover better seating arrangements, more effective use of space, or more pleasing color schemes. We buy new plants, new artwork, and if needed, additional furnishings. It's a fun-filled, lighthearted day that renews both our work space and our spirits. Everyone gets involved, which creates a sense of ownership and pride in each person that would not exist if he or she had not personally participated. In the end, this turns out to be a relationship-building event as well as a clean-up day.

Careful Planning Pays Off

To achieve optimum results, you must plan carefully

During Learning Forum's "Office Beautification Day," the office is rearranged, replenished, and renewed as a working space.

VAROOOM

which elements to use in your office environment. Keep in mind the ultimate purpose that each section of the office serves. For example, you'll want lightweight tables and chairs for rooms where furniture will be rearranged frequently to suit changing needs. Lozanov stresses using:

- Lots of plants to create a more soothing atmosphere;
- Natural lighting whenever possible; and
- Full-spectrum lighting that can be made softer or brighter depending upon the need.

Our office has both skylights and track lighting. The track lights allow us to control the direction as well as the intensity of the light. Employees who previously complained of headaches from our old fluorescent lights found great relief when we changed to natural lighting and full-spectrum lamps.

What you hang on the walls also says a great deal about who you are. We take advantage of this opportunity to send a strong message about our organization by hanging our vision statement at the office entrance. It's one of the first things customers see when they walk in. After reading the statement, many of them mention that they're moved by the vision. We want people to know up-front what we stand for and why we're in business. As a result, they're more relaxed and receptive when we meet face-to-face.

We also showcase our past, present, and future on the walls, displaying SuperCamp brochures, photos, and charts of current and future projects. The photos of past staff, students, and programs and the increasing sophistication of our brochures make our history visible and keep us aware of who we are and how we began. It also helps us keep the "big picture" of our overall business in mind.

The one room in which we don't have anything on the walls is our conference room. There the walls are covered

Carefully plan office elements to optimize your work and energy levels.

Display your:

Vision statement

::

Photos

::

Awards

::

Brochures of past products
and services

with whiteboards for planning and note-taking. It's a fine example of a room designed with its end-use in mind. The room gracefully manages to serve many purposes. Large enough for group activities as well as formal meetings with the entire office, it's furnished with one large table, comfortable chairs that can be arranged throughout the room, track lighting that can be dimmed for different moods, and skylights for natural light. Flip-chart stands, a stereo system, a television, and a VCR complete the setup. When used in conjunction with our fully-equipped kitchen for providing meals and refreshments, this room is ideal for small seminars and training sessions.

The design and details of an office should reflect how you do business. At Learning Forum, we avoid meeting across a desk, as this puts one person in a position of implied dominance over the other. We prefer to meet seated in circles or at a round table. This arrangement puts everyone on the same level and encourages cooperation and participation. Meeting without a table also makes people more open and less likely to "hide" from the rest of the group.

The overall plan of our office is open, with a feeling of spaciousness. We feel this design encourages cooperation and open-mindedness. We avoid using walls and cubicles so as to facilitate teamwork among departments. By limiting the use of dividers, we make it easier for staff to see one another and communicate. Staff members find themselves much more likely to discuss problems, find new solutions, and work as a team when there's easy access between departments. Not only is the furniture in the conference room movable so as to create small, more intimate meeting areas, but each department also has areas set up with a small table and comfortable chairs.

By meeting in a circle and without a desk or table, individual participation, openness, and cooperation are encouraged.

Keeping Physically Fit

Quantum Business includes keeping your body in shape as well as your mind. Today, some large companies are including gyms, pools, or running tracks in their floor plans. This may not be feasible for a smaller organization, but we found that we were able to encourage exercise simply by installing a shower. Some of our employees bike or jog to work or exercise at a nearby gym—something they wouldn't do if they didn't have a place to clean up afterward.

If you have the space, you can also hold exercise classes during lunch or after-hours. We once had an employee who taught aerobics courses in his spare time, and was kind enough to offer step-training classes in our conference room. By the way, these activities are initiated by our staff. No one is told to exercise; they simply take advantage of the resources that are provided. The desire for self-improvement must come from within, and that starts with a supportive environment. I believe all people have a desire to fulfill their potential, and only need the opportunities and support to do so.

Reinventing the Business Meeting

First-time visitors to our office are often surprised by what they find. A few years ago, a large corporation was looking for a nonprofit organization to sponsor. One of their candidates was our Learning Forum Foundation, which provides, among other things, scholarships for students who can't afford SuperCamp. Several of the corporation's executives flew in from Chicago for an early-morning meeting with us.

The men arrived dressed in their dark suits and ties, briefcases in hand, and serious expressions on their faces. I remember how shocked they looked when they got to the

First-time visitors to Learning Forum are sometimes surprised by what they find.

front door and saw the large "WELCOME" sign hanging over it. We greeted them in our SuperCamp T-shirts, smiling, and playing upbeat music. This was obviously not at all what they had expected.

Entering the office, they found a table laden with fruit, muffins, coffee, and juice. Signs with statements like "Whatever I Dream, I Can Become" decorated the walls. Whiteboards and flip charts with sets of brightly colored pens were ready for presentations. Instead of meeting formally at the conference table, we had arranged the chairs in an intimate circle.

We also had someone at a computer taking notes throughout the meeting and creating charts and other materials. When the sessions ended five hours later, our visitors took with them notes of all that was said, as well as a complete project plan. They left with smiles on their faces and a bounce in their step.

The executives experienced who we are and what we value. They saw by our actions and environment that we believe in positive, joyful, meaningful relationships and an uplifting work environment. Though because of a funding cutback the corporation eventually decided not to sponsor any organization, one of the men who visited that day was so moved that he made a personal gift to the Foundation and has donated faithfully every year since.

What those managers experienced that day was a shift in their thinking about how a business could be run. Our conduct of the meeting was just one example of taking a standard business practice and reinventing it. The meeting elements—environment, atmosphere, relationships—are a part of every office, but are often ignored or left to chance. But at Learning Forum, the elements are carefully thought out and created.

Visitors who are unfamiliar with SuperCamp aren't the only ones surprised by our approach to meetings. Even our summer staff is sometimes caught off guard. Not long ago, a staff member from the East Coast visited San Diego and we invited her to stop by the office. She showed up in professional attire, ready to meet the "corporate bigwigs." Instead, she was greeted by people dressed comfortably in slacks and shirts. As she toured the office, brightened by skylights in the beamed ceiling and decorated with camp photos and plants, her ideas of what an office had to be started to break down.

Later she described her experience like this: "Music started blasting over the intercom and someone grabbed me by the arm and pulled me into a meeting with the whole company. Everyone stood in a circle and the structure was similar to meetings we had at our summer programs. So was the atmosphere. They talked as much about personal issues and the new experiences they enjoyed over the weekend as they did about business. But there was an agenda and there was direction. It's just that these things were part of the agenda. Fifteen minutes later, the meeting was over and the music started again. The mood was upbeat and happy even though there was a lot of work to be done. It wasn't what I'd pictured, but it makes sense. If this is where SuperCamp is created, then what we feel is important for creating a positive, productive atmosphere at our summer programs should be done here as well."

The similarities between SuperCamp and Learning Forum are no accident. We operate on a strong foundation that permeates all aspects of our business. If there's one action that has more impact than any other on both business success and personal satisfaction, it's the laying of a strong foundation. By that I mean clarifying the principles and values by which you live and holding a powerful vision of where you're headed.

Putting What You Do into Context

At Burklyn, we considered it very important to distinguish between "context" and "content." Marshall Thurber liked to explain the difference this way: Imagine a bowl filled with fruit. The bowl is the context, that which holds everything together. Our vision, principles, values, beliefs, and culture define our environment and our actions. They set the context of our lives. The fruit is the content. It's what we do and make. In the case of Learning Forum, the content includes SuperCamp, the videos we produce, the training seminars we offer, and all the other things we do.

An organization's context incorporates those things that form its philosophical foundation. The tighter and stronger the context (the bowl), the more the staff members are held in alignment. To that extent, their efficiency and effectiveness increase and the company experiences greater success. Buckminster Fuller even created a word to describe this phenomenon. "Synergy," he said, "is created when the whole is greater than the sum of its parts." When context is loose and company principles are not clearly defined, the foundation (the bowl) is weak, and everyone holds a different vision, or no vision, resulting in ineffective, frustrated staff, and an unproductive organization.

As someone who has worked for years developing our company vision, I continue to marvel at its power. Perhaps the most difficult part of the process is creating the vision statement itself. Crafting that statement forces us to carefully formulate and clarify our views. I've found the vision statement to be a valuable tool for inspiring us and keeping all of us motivated. It reminds us of our reason for being in

The fruit bowl analogy distinguishes context and content.

business. It keeps us from getting sidetracked and spending valuable resources on inappropriate projects.

Vision gives the staff a deeper reason for coming to work every day, a reason that goes beyond the paycheck. It adds meaning to daily activities and gives us all a sense of purpose and fulfillment. It gives us a psychological anchor that we can grab hold of, so that when something happens that's in line with the vision, we can say, "Yes! That's why I'm here."

A powerful vision of what could be gives us a direction in which to move and the motivation to change our present situation. When we clearly see where we want to be (our vision), and have carefully examined where we are now, we begin to be pulled toward the vision. Our actions take on meaning and purpose that naturally move us forward. Without vision, there's nothing to beckon us, to urge us on.

This does not mean that what has gone before is without value. In fact, to clarify our vision, we need an accurate picture of the past. At Learning Forum, part of formulating our company vision statement involved taking a hard look at our past and present, then projecting ourselves ten years into the future. We did this at an office meeting that involved the entire staff. It turned out to be a day that literally reshaped our future.

We'd been working on our vision statement for some time, but it seemed abstract and unreal. That day, we gave it substance.

The Future Comes Alive

First, we discussed our company history and our present situation. Sitting together in a circle, we shared memories of the past. We created charts depicting political and business trends. We relived our history through stories and old photographs until everyone clearly understood our past,

To clarify a vision, start with an accurate picture of the present and knowledge of the past.

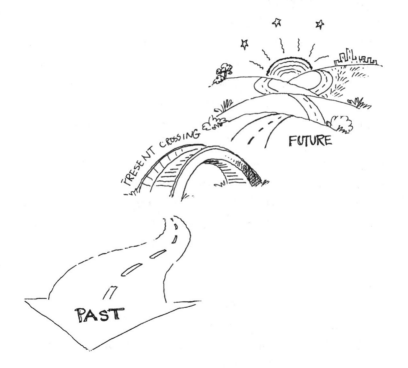

where we had "come from," and our present, where we were that day.

Then we broke up into small groups of three or four and began mapping out our future, each group focusing on a different area of the company. Using long sheets of butcher paper with a grid along the top measuring out the years, we recorded future milestones.

Projecting into the future was difficult. At first we moved cautiously, but as we got further into the process the momentum picked up and we grew more excited and imaginative. Our motto became "Anything goes," and we began shouting out seemingly crazy ideas like "teleporting to summer sites; a SuperCamp movie; a Learning Forum television show." Since that day, some of these "crazy ideas" have become reality. Programs in Southeast Asia, a book on Quantum Learning, and an international Quantum Learning conference each grew out of the brainstorming we did that day. I'm convinced these things would not have happened without this effort, for if we had not taken the time to envision these projects, how could we have moved toward making them a reality?

After nearly two years of deep consideration of our purpose, and much rewriting, we arrived at a vision statement that truly describes our company and has stood the test of time.

It reads:

An international model of excellence,

facilitating a shift in learning,

resulting in creative, educated, responsible people,

participating in the global community.

A Matter of Principle

Learning Forum is built on our vision. The process of

formulating that vision brought to light other important elements of our context—our principles and values.

Webster's dictionary defines a principle as "1. an accepted or professed rule of action or conduct; 2. a fundamental law, axiom, or doctrine." Principles like honesty, charity, and justice are external, constant, and exist throughout society.

For Quantum Learning, we've adapted, refined, and added to these principles. We call them the 8 Keys of Excellence, and following these keys has created a positive and productive environment at Learning Forum. We believe in these principles, internalize them, and make them a part of our professional and personal lives.

The 8 Keys of Excellence are at the heart of the Quantum Learning foundation. They direct us to act in ways that support and respect others. By living these principles, we create an open, trusting, supportive environment. We'll examine each key in depth in later chapters.

At SuperCamp we've learned the 8 Keys are most effective when woven throughout the course. On the first day of each program, we give a brief definition of the Keys. Then each day for the rest of the week we have a "Key for the Day," and explain in detail why that key is important.

Because people learn in different ways, we use a wide variety of methods to teach the keys. Then we repeat the information to cement it into long-term memory. Students may be asked to write, create and perform skits, listen to stories, draw pictures, or participate in other activities that will help them remember the material. Dr. Lozanov developed this method of interweaving psychological concepts into the content of a course to make learning more effective. I'm going to use the same approach for this book, alternating "Key" chapters with chapters on learning techniques. This will help cement the information in your memory and will balance content with context.

The 8 Keys of Excellence can make a dramatic difference in your personal and professional life. Organizations that follow these keys become more supportive, open, and friendly. They become places where people learn, grow, discover solutions, develop innovative products, and work together as a team.

Adopt the 8 Keys into your business and your life and they'll put you on the road to achieving Quantum success.

Values—It's What's Inside that Counts

Unlike principles, which are external and unchanging, values and beliefs are internal, personal, and different for everyone. You may value family ties, education, and good health, for example, while your boss values hard work, loyalty, and dedication to duty. According to Stephen Covey, author of *Principle-Centered Leadership* (Summit Books, New York, 1991), our values and beliefs develop throughout childhood and are shaped by culture and family. "These [values] become the 'glasses' through which we look at the world. We evaluate, assign priorities, judge, and behave based on how we see life through these glasses."

For any organization to be successful, the employees' personal values must be aligned with the company's values. If not, the employees soon become uncomfortable in the environment, and must either change their views or leave.

At Learning Forum, we dedicate meetings to clarifying our company and personal values and beliefs, and we've found it extremely valuable to put these convictions in writing. We also communicate our principles and values in

Learning Forum's 8 Keys of Excellence are at the heart of Quantum Learning.

Live in Integrity
Conduct yourself in the state of authenticity, sincerity, and wholeness that results when your values and behavior are aligned.

Acknowledge that Failure Leads to Success
Understand failures simply provide us with the information we need to learn so we can succeed.

Speak with Good Purpose
Develop the skill of speaking in a positive sense, being responsible for honest and direct communication.

Live in the Now—This Is It!
Develop the ability to focus your attention on the present moment. Each moment, each task counts.

Affirm Your Commitment
Follow your vision without wavering; stay true to the course. Do whatever it takes to get the job done.

Take Ownership
Be accountable and responsible. Be someone who can be counted upon, someone who responds.

Stay Flexible
Maintain the ability to change what you are doing to get the outcome you desire.

Keep Your Balance
Maintain your mind, body and spirit in alignment.

our company literature. It's a statement of who we are. We find that many of the things we believe in, such as positive relationships, are related to our principles (see Speak with Good Purpose, Chapter 3).

Part of the context of Learning Forum is our belief that positive relationships are paramount. Good relationships move us forward; poor relationships hold us back. When people work joyfully together they accomplish far more than when they are at odds. They focus on making things happen, achieving goals, improving systems, or inventing new products. At Learning Forum, strong relationships mean co-workers feel safe and trusting. They bounce ideas off one another without fear of criticism, communicate their concerns clearly and effectively, and develop programs and products free of any fears of failure. Personally and professionally, they keep growing.

Of course, personality types also have something to do with how well people get along. You may think that working well with your co-workers means you're lucky. You may also believe that when you and your co-workers don't get along there's nothing you can do. Both are misconceptions. It may surprise you to learn how much environment and communication skills, also part of the context, can contribute to and greatly influence the outcome of relationships. When context is tight—when we value good relationships and principles like "Speak with Good Purpose"—we experience alignment with and positive feelings about each other, which leads to synergy.

Our behavior is directed by our context, and the more we model this behavior, the more it spreads throughout the company. It's an on-going process.

If you recall the fruit bowl analogy, the bowl is made up of our vision, principles, and values. That's our *context*.

For any organization to be successful, the employees' personal values must be aligned with the company's values.

66 *Values and beliefs develop throughout childhood and are shaped by culture and family.* *99*

— Stephen R. Covey
   Author, *Principle-Centered Leadership*

The *contents* of the bowl are the things we do, our programs and products. Our company mission is to create environments and resources for lifelong learning and personal success. A strong context allows our work, our content, to be completed more effectively. Staff members can focus on their jobs because they have a clear picture of the rules we play by and the direction we're headed. We can see this at Learning Forum in the strong sense of teamwork and cooperation. We rarely stay within the confines of our job descriptions. Reaching company goals or completing the task at hand comes first.

Vision Meetings: A Day to Focus

We do our best to make our context a part of each day, but the one day we focus completely on it is at our annual Vision Meeting. If you plan to create a shift in your company culture, a vision meeting may be just the place to start.

Our Vision Meeting is a day-long, all-staff affair that focuses on where we've been, where we are now, and where we want to go. We immerse ourselves in the ultimate Quantum Learning environment, so that we may hold that picture in our minds as a reminder of what we're all about.

We've held Vision Meetings both on-site and at outside locations, since it's sometimes good to get out of the office. One memorable meeting was held in a conference room on a bluff overlooking the ocean. The wall facing the sea was all window, and as the staff entered they were greeted by a stunning view of waves breaking on the shore below. We arranged our chairs around this large window, using the ocean as the backdrop for the meeting. We also decorated the room with inspirational posters, plants, and flowers, and we played a variety of music to create different moods. Creating the atmosphere you want through such details is important. It helps you set the direction and tone of the meeting.

The activities vary each year depending on what we feel is needed. However, essential elements always include reviewing the vision statement, discussing our past, present, and future, and building relationships.

We often begin our meeting by reading the company vision statement. Sometimes we take turns discussing what it means to us or sharing our own personal visions. This is a time to check in and make sure we are all aligned and heading in the right direction—that we are truly pursuing our vision. The amount of time we spend on this exercise depends on how aligned we are as a group.

At one meeting, when we were discussing our roots, I shared stories about the Burklyn Business School. It was an intensely personal experience for me. Munching on cookies, we gathered around the television and watched my old video on the "Story of Burklyn." The film was shot in the late 1970's, during the height of our business school, and I had not sat down and watched it in many years.

I was moved by the faces of the past, the beautiful mansion and surrounding acres of countryside, and the joy and inspiration we had felt in that place. We were pioneers exploring new methods of teaching and learning. As we watched the film, I saw inspired students who have since moved on to become successful business owners. I saw the room where Buckminster Fuller used to teach. And I remembered the favorite places where my children liked to play.

I told our staff that the concepts for our 8 Keys had their origins in this place, as well as many of the activities that are part of SuperCamp. I believe it gave them a better understanding of the roots of our company and of who I am as well. It also brought us closer together as a group. Our yearly vision meetings are casual, friendly, and relaxed. Relationships are deepened when you share something of yourself and your company history.

The staff looks forward to them with anticipation, since most of them don't know the agenda (we keep it a surprise to create momentum). But there's no fear of what might happen. It's a friendly, inspiring, focused gathering. We serve muffins, juice, and coffee in the morning and lunch in the afternoon. Many of our seasoned staff show up in sweats or jeans.

To help solidify the feeling of being a team, when we have a Vision Meeting, we have a group photo taken at the end of the day. Copies of the photo are framed, with the vision statement written beneath it, and put on each desk. We also give each person a gift to remember the day, such as the "Team Learning Forum" sweatshirts that were given at our last meeting as a special surprise for the staff. This is fun for everyone and gives us a feeling of unity and team spirit.

The power of a strong foundation, or context, can make an incredible difference in your company. It facilitates alignment, teamwork, direction, and action. If you're the key person in your company, take time now to examine your vision, principles, and values; you'll begin to lay the foundation for your success. If you don't have a vision statement, put it on your priority list. If you do have one, look at it and ask yourself if it still reflects what your company is about. If it doesn't, start rewriting it, or suggest a company Vision Meeting so everyone can participate in the task. If it's fine the way it is, ask yourself if everyone

Vision Meeting agendas are flexible enough to change from year to year.

A sample agenda:

All staff seated in a circle

- Welcome and opening thoughts
- Exploration and reading of vision statement
- Activity to make vision more personally meaningful
- Story of your business (past)
- Review of principles and beliefs
- Communication circle
  (Each person tells a personal story relating to principles and beliefs)
- Relationships/Team-Building activity
- Review of the past year leading to current situation
- Activity reports, financial reports, etc.
- Paint a picture of where the company wants to be in five to ten years
- Activity to co-create this along with yearly milestones
- Discuss/plan year ahead, roles of employees, activities, and goals
- Group photo (Later framed with vision/mission statement for each employee)
- Give gift along with inspirational words
- Closing party

knows the statement and is aligned on it. If not, take it upon yourself to see that they are.

If you're not in a position to spearhead these kinds of moves, talk to the person in your company who is, and offer to help them get started. I cannot imagine a company officer who would not be delighted by your interest and high-mindedness. And when the executive sees the benefits your work produces, who knows how much that will raise the value of your personal stock?

Celebrate Your Learning!

! *How does your physical space affect how you learn?*

A carefully controlled environment can help you feel relaxed and at ease, making you more receptive to learning.

! *How can you plan your office environment so as to create a positive impact on your work?*

First, keep in mind the ultimate purpose of each section of your office. Use lots of plants to create a more soothing atmosphere and natural lighting whenever possible.

! *What can you do to transform meetings from boring to exciting, from wasteful to productive?*

Make the tone and format of your meetings match the purpose and values of your organization. Meet at a circular table, or sit in a circle, so all participants are equal. Keep the atmosphere safe, positive, and supportive.

! *What is the role of "vision" in your organization's future?*

Vision helps you create a clear picture of where you want to be in the future. A powerful vision drives you and directs your actions.

3

Success Is Built
on Relationships;
Relationships Are Built
on Communication

 *What is the biggest problem
in the workplace?*

 *What does "Speak with Good
Purpose" mean and why is it
important to your life and work?*

 *What is "Active Listening" and how
can it help you?*

 *What's the best way to apologize
to a customer or co-worker?*

I t takes more than just a healthy, well-planned physical environment to create success. A company's emotional environment is just as important. As we saw in Chapter 2, positive relationships among co-workers are critical. Employee fear and mistrust results in poor service for the customer and slow business for the owner.

Dr. W. Edwards Deming, best known for promoting quality in the workplace by continually improving systems, once said, "The biggest problem in the workplace is fear."

Fear causes a shutdown of initiative and creativity. Research in neuroscience has shown that sections of the brain called the midbrain or limbic system influence our emotions by releasing hormones that govern our physiological state. Stress and fear induce chemical changes in the brain that distort perception and hamper its ability to process information. In a workplace where fear is used to keep people in line and to get the most out of them, actually the opposite occurs. Employees become immobilized by fear and care little about the quality of their work. This results in poor performance and high turnover.

At Learning Forum, to combat fear, we do our best to build a positive emotional environment. When there's safety, trust, and joy in the workplace, people function at a higher level, leading them to be loyal, hardworking, creative, and willing to do whatever it takes to get the job done.

The success of our Spirit of SuperCamp events is the result of staff taking pride in the outcome. Some stay in the office until midnight or longer, working out the details of curriculum, painting posters, and collating papers. They're not required to do this, but they believe in their work, find joy in it, and care enough to make sure every detail is done right. This sort of dedication can't be found in a workplace dominated by fear.

The key to building a joyful, safe, and meaningful work-place is to create inclusion and build relationships. "Inclusion" means making sure that everyone has a sense of the significance of what they're doing and a feeling of belonging to the organization. In a very large company, this may have to be done department by department, but it's important to have everyone pulling together as much as possible, from the CEO to the data entry person.

One way we create inclusion is through our daily check-in meetings (mentioned in Chapter 2) where we share important information and personal news. At these meet-ings, the entire company meets for about 15 minutes at the same time each day. Upbeat music signals the beginning and end of the meeting. To keep it from running on too long, we stand in a circle instead of sitting. This brief get-together lets us take a moment to realign, ask questions, bring up new ideas or air assumptions. It's an open forum for anyone who wants to speak. We take turns running the meeting and taking notes for those not present. The agenda is:

1. "Burning Shares"
   Personal or business items you're excited about and want to share;

2. "FYI"
   Business-related information; and

3. "Focus"
   Areas demanding special attention and any needs for support people might have that day.

We also start and close our meetings with traditions. Most associations and clubs, like Girl Scouts, Elks, and

Rotary, have specific traditions that help create a sense of belonging and security. At Learning Forum we also have a number of traditions that we carefully preserve. For our meetings, we have a tradition called "bringing it in" and "letting it go." Our brains like clean beginnings and clean endings. Quantum Learning uses movement to help the brain remember and store information, and traditions help anchor that information in our minds. At the start of each new meeting, we play upbeat music and "bring it in" by swinging one arm down in an arc, as if pounding a gavel. At the end of the swing, we snap our fingers and the music is abruptly turned off. When a meeting or topic is complete, we "bring it out" by swinging the imaginary gavel in the opposite direction (up), and as we snap again, the music goes on. When we swing our arms down to bring it in, our minds connect this movement with the start of the meeting and put us in an alert, focused state. When we "bring it out," we take our focus off the new information and are ready to move on to the rest of the day.

Short check-in meetings like these are especially useful at our busiest times. They allow everyone to join together and to further relationships by sharing things that are exciting. They also provide a way for employees to get support when they need it. Everyone also has an opportunity to brainstorm, present new ideas, and offer solutions to problems others need help with.

About once a month, we have an hour-long meeting to update the entire staff on the company's progress. Plus, we regularly plan company lunches, parties, and activities that encourage communication and strengthen relationships. We even have an employee whose job description includes "Social Director." By having someone responsible for these events, we make sure they take place. In many organiza-

Traditions create a sense of belonging and security.

*One tradition is "bringing in" and "letting go"
a meeting with a finger snap.*

tions, this task is done haphazardly, if at all. But we consider them part of our tradition and give them the importance they deserve. Traditions such as these activities and playing music to signal the beginning and end of meetings help unify us.

Building strong relationships is an ongoing process. I used to think that simply working on relationship problems when they came up would be enough. I soon learned that it isn't. You can't have a smooth-running car if all you do is fix it when it breaks down. You have to do preventive maintenance—change the oil, etc. In business, you must make it part of the emotional environment to constantly develop and maintain strong relationships.

We recently hired several new employees. To get to know them better, we held a luncheon. Because we have a full kitchen, luncheons are something we can do quite often at low cost and without having to leave the building. We always involve everyone in deciding the menu and contributing to the meal by preparing items at home and bringing them to the office. Our meals run the gamut from salad bars, tacos, burritos, and sandwiches to complete spaghetti dinners. At one holiday party we even cooked a turkey! However, the meal needn't be extravagant to be enjoyable. Something about sitting down together and sharing food we've all prepared generates feelings of community and belonging.

At our luncheon for the new employees, we passed around a hat filled with slips of paper. Each slip had a different question printed on it. Things like "What's your favorite animal at the zoo, and why?" "What's your dream vacation?" As we took turns answering the questions, we all got more comfortable.

Luncheons are great ice-breakers for both new and

established people. It's a perfect starting place to begin building positive relationships, and it sends the message that strong relationships are part of the "context" at Learning Forum. We celebrate birthdays, holidays, and important company achievements like record-breaking enrollments for our programs. Sometimes, we just have spontaneous lunchtime pizza parties or buy submarine sandwiches. The cost is small and makes for a more joyful workplace.

Speak with Good Purpose

While activities like parties and luncheons bring people together, they're not enough to ensure that the people will build strong relationships. Gossip, complaints, insults, and other forms of negative communication, if prevalent, will eventually destroy a healthy environment. Negative communication is extremely damaging. Staff members must learn to avoid gossip, address grievances and concerns in a mature manner, and express themselves clearly and directly. That's why we consider the Key of Excellence, Speak with Good Purpose, to be the cornerstone of healthy relationships.

Speak with Good Purpose means communicate with positive intent; make it honest and direct. Avoid repeating or encouraging negative comments and gossip. Instead, focus on positive conversation and solutions. To do this, you must tell the truth, air assumptions, and maintain integrity by apologizing when necessary.

Marshall Thurber used to introduce this Key at Burklyn by reading the following passage from a book called *Rolling Thunder,* by Doug Boyd (Random House, New York, 1974). In it, Rolling Thunder, a Native American, describes the values and principles of his culture.

"People have to be responsible for their thoughts, so they

have to learn to control them. It may not be easy, but it can be done. First of all, if we don't want to think certain things we don't say them. We don't have to eat everything we see, and we don't have to say everything we think. So we begin by watching our words and speaking with good purpose only. There are times when we must have clear and pure minds with no unwanted thoughts and we have to train and prepare steadily for those times until we are ready. We don't have to say or think what we don't wish to. We have a choice in those things, and we have to realize that and practice using that choice. There is no use condemning yourself for the thoughts and ideas and dreams that come into your mind; so there's no use arguing with yourself or fighting your thoughts. Just realize that you can think what you choose. You don't have to pay any attention to those unwanted thoughts. If they keep coming into your head, just leave them alone and say, 'I don't choose to have such thoughts,' and they will soon go away. If you keep a steady determination and stick with that purpose you will know how to use that choice and control your consciousness so unwanted thoughts don't come to you anymore."

You have the power to choose positive, powerful thoughts or negative, damaging thoughts. The first step is becoming aware of the negative thoughts that pop into your mind. Think about that little voice in your head, the one that says, "You can't because . . . ," the one that comes up with reasons why you will fail before you even try. What you say to yourself greatly affects your confidence. You may be blocking yourself from starting your own business, asking for a raise, changing careers, or leading your company effectively because of the confidence being sapped from you by the negative things you tell yourself. Even words as seemingly innocent as "I'll never be able to finish this on time" affect your confidence in yourself.

At SuperCamp we ask students, "What would you do if you knew you couldn't fail?" Ask yourself that question now. What is it that's holding you back? Is it that voice in your head, insisting it's impossible, impractical, and dangerous to take a risk? Exert control over that voice, and begin telling yourself how you will succeed. As Rolling Thunder tells us, "We have a choice in those things, and we have to realize and practice using that choice." Make the choice to speak to yourself with good purpose.

You also need to listen carefully to how you speak to other people. Ask yourself, "Are my words encouraging and useful, or damaging?" Notice the tone of voice you use. Do you sound as if you're whining, defeated, or complaining, no matter what you're talking about? We sometimes unconsciously adopt patterns of speech that hamper our ability to communicate clearly. Once you're aware of a communication problem, you can begin to focus on change. You can choose to Speak with Good Purpose only, rather than saying whatever comes to mind. We don't need to say everything that comes to mind.

At Learning Forum we use several communication tools to help us solve conflicts and "Speak with Good Purpose." They include the following:

Active Listening

Visible Communication ("Open The Front Door")

Four-Part Apology

You may be thinking that Speak with Good Purpose works great as long as everyone is getting along, but when things go awry, the old habits come back. Well, it's true, when you have a disagreement with someone, it can be difficult to clearly communicate your feelings without slipping into negative patterns like laying blame or attacking with a barrage of angry insults and accusations.

But that approach only leads to confusion, disappointment, hurt feelings, and even fights. You can, however, use good communication skills to discuss disagreements clearly and without upset. This will bring understanding and will help you work together to devise solutions on which you both agree.

Active Listening

You may have overheard two people talking about something and noticed that neither one was listening to the other. Each one is busy lecturing, advising, or defending his or her position, but the conversation never moves toward resolution. Both talkers are mired deep in their own opinions, spinning their wheels, and going nowhere. At SuperCamp we call this "getting stuck in muck."

On a farm, muck is a mixture of dirt, water, and manure. It's thick, sticky, sinks underfoot, and keeps you from moving forward. When you muck a conversation, you impede productive communication by denying the feelings the other person is trying to express. Some examples of mucking include the following:

Reassurance
"Oh, you don't need to lose weight, you look great the way you are."

Giving Advice
"If you're having so much trouble juggling work and family obligations, what you need to do is take a time management course."

"Mucking" a conversation impedes productive communication by denying other people's feelings.

"Mucking" includes:

Reassurance

::

Advice

::

Identification

Identification

> "The same thing happened to me when I was . . . "
> Or interrupting and saying, "I know exactly what
> you mean; I also . . . " Meanwhile, the speaker never
> gets a chance to finish what he wanted to say.

Other common ways to muck a conversation are being
defensive, asking leading questions that divert the conversation from what the person is trying to communicate or
playing "top this": "When I did it, it was much harder . . . "

Usually we respond this way in a well-meaning attempt
to relate to the other person or help solve his problems.
Instead we end up closing the door on the conversation.
The purpose of listening is to understand, not to solve problems, convince, lecture, or advise.

Active Listening is the art of listening attentively to
someone and letting him know he has been heard. It is the
practice of seeing the situation through the other person's
eyes. Stephen Covey, in his book, *7 Habits of Highly
Effective People* (Simon and Schuster, New York, 1989. All
rights reserved.), says, "Seek first to understand, then to be
understood." Look your co-worker in the eye while he's
speaking. Let him complete his thoughts or his version of
an incident without interruption. Absorb what he's saying
and try to truly understand him. Don't use this time to
formulate your own thoughts or arguments. When your co-
worker is finished speaking, paraphrase what was just said
to make sure you understand it. For example, "What I think
you're saying is, you believe it's important that we work on
this project before the one I proposed because you believe
it will cost less, be more timely, and make our customer
happier." Only after your co-worker says, "Yes, that's what
I'm saying," or something similar, do you give your point of
view. We call this "earning the right to speak." You earn the

"right" only after you've truly understood the other person's point of view. Only then will your co-worker feel heard and be more likely to listen attentively to your thoughts. This helps when your goal is to reach an agreement.

Visible Communication

This is the practice of stating everything clearly, with no hidden agenda. When you use this technique, your partner doesn't have to fill in the blanks and possibly misinterpret what you're saying.

How many times have you been asked, "Are you free tonight?" or "What are you doing tomorrow?" You have no idea if the person is asking you to do something fun or is gearing up to ask you for a favor. Depending upon which it is, your answer might be completely different. But since the intent of the question is "invisible," you feel manipulated and possibly even trapped.

How much better for the questioner to say, "I have two tickets to a play tonight. Are you free to go with me?" Or, "I need help on my project and wanted to know if you were free tonight and willing to help me with it."

Then you can answer the question knowing what you are committing to and it doesn't make you feel uncomfortable and awkward. Even a simple question like, "How did you like the movie?" has problem potential. If you say you loved it, will the questioner respond that he thought it was the worst movie he's ever seen? That's why it's always best to say what you mean, and let others know your intentions.

OTFD: Open The Front Door

At SuperCamp, we use the acronym OTFD (Open The Front Door) to teach clear, visible communication to students. OTFD is especially powerful in communicating an upset. It includes the following steps:

The Letter "O" Stands for Observation

Begin by describing something you observed with your senses that anyone else could observe. For example: "You didn't show up for our meeting this morning."

The "T" Is for Thought

State your thoughts or opinion on what you observed. "I thought you forgot it or didn't feel it was important."

The "F" Stands for Feeling

Give your feelings about what you observed. "When you didn't show, I felt angry and frustrated."

The "D" Is for Desire

Describe what you desire about the situation. "If you find you can't make it to a meeting, I want you to notify me a day before or as soon as you know."

This approach may seem simplistic, but breaking down your communication into these four segments enables you to separate what actually happened from your feelings about the incident, and then come to an understanding. Many problems can be easily resolved without leaving the other person hanging, not knowing what to say, or feeling the need to justify and defend a position. Usually, you'll find that when you finish the conversation with what you desire, the person you're speaking to will simply agree. In the above example, he might say, "Yes, I know that must have been upsetting and my intention in the future is to let you know if I can't make a meeting." OTFD is not only useful when you're upset, it also helps you to simply be clear in any communication.

Specific strategies are useful for clear communication.

Open The Front Door

O bservation
Describe something you observed

T hought
State your thoughts or opinions
on what you observed

F eeling
Give your feelings on
what you observed

D esire
Describe what you desire
about the situation

Four-Part Apology

Apologizing when you've made a mistake isn't easy. When you're in that situation, however, the Four-Part Apology can help. It allows you to acknowledge what you did, take responsibility for it, and look beyond the actual incident to the consequences of your behavior. By stating those consequences and choosing a different behavior, you can help the person you have affected move from feeling angry or resentful to being thoughtful and supportive.

First, Acknowledge What You've Done

Take responsibility for your actions by admitting them. Use "I" statements when speaking. "I acknowledge that I disrupted your plans and hurt your feelings when I missed the meeting."

Second, Apologize

During this step, state the cost or damage your actions caused. "I apologize for hurting you and wasting your time by making you wait for me."

Third, Make It Right

Deal with the consequences of the behavior and offer a solution. "I know you spent half an hour waiting for me. Is there a project I can help you with to make up the lost time?"

Fourth, Recommit

Make a commitment to appropriate behavior. "I agree to be on time or call in advance if I can't make it."

Following these steps makes it easier for both parties to focus on the behavior rather than the person. By taking responsibility for the action, you sidestep opportunities to lay blame on some outside force or circumstance using

When apologizing for your mistakes, take responsibility for your actions

Four-Part Apology

1. Acknowledge

Take responsibility for your actions and behaviors; use "I" statements

2. Apologize

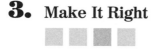

Apologize and acknowledge the "cost" to others; if unaware, ask

3. Make It Right

Deal with the consequences of behavior; ask the person, "Is there anything I can do?"

4. Recommit

Make a commitment to appropriate behavior

excuses such as, "I'm really sorry. You know it wasn't my fault I was late. Traffic is always heavy early in the morning. That's why I was late."

All of the communication skills discussed here can help you and your co-workers work out differences more effectively and come to workable solutions. It's going to take some training and practice, and may feel awkward at first. In fact, you may want to hold an office communication training session and practice OTFD and the Four-Part Apology in mock disagreements and arguments. In a training or role-playing situation, I recommend you have a third party listen in, since much can be gained from getting an outside perspective. These techniques will become more natural and easy to use as you practice them over time. You will definitely see a difference in your relationships at home and in the office. Everyone will feel more open and relaxed when you and your colleagues realize you have the power to clarify miscommunications and reduce upsets.

Yes, these skills and techniques are simple; some would even call them hokey. But they work, and the effect is so powerful, they produce results that often seem like magic. Sometimes people will be at odds for years over a small miscommunication which, when cleared up, releases positive energy, creates synergy, and gets an organization moving fast-forward. Don't take my word for it. Try it in your department, or your company, and see.

Getting Outside Help

When there are deeper, ongoing differences between employees, you might consider counseling sessions to work things out. Once we hired two staff members to work closely, but they couldn't seem to get along. Both had applied for the same position, and this created tension between them. Sharon—the one who didn't get it—felt resentful, and the other, Louise, seemed insensitive to Sharon's feelings. Since they hadn't spent much time getting to know each other more personally, their feelings were based solely on a working relationship. Since they were unable to communicate clearly, differences built up and the tension increased until Sharon was ready to quit. We didn't want to lose either person, so we decided to get some outside help. We contacted a professional counselor, and they both agreed to see him.

It was time and money well spent. I don't know if it was what the counselor said to them or their realization that good relationships were obviously so important to us that we would pay $150 an hour to have someone meet with them, but Sharon and Louise left the first session together laughing and smiling. The transformation was phenomenal. They discovered they each had different ways of approaching and handling conflicts and they were misinterpreting these differences as personal attacks.

"I wanted to talk a problem out immediately," Sharon said, "but Louise wanted to think about it first, then discuss it. This drove me crazy. I was frustrated at how long it took and I thought she was avoiding me. I wasn't considering her feelings; I just wanted to get things done."

Recognizing their differences helped Sharon and Louise understand each other better and gave them a starting point from which to begin building a new relationship. "We realized we respected each other and wanted to make things work," Louise told me. It didn't take them long to become good friends, and they've been working together successfully now for many years.

This is not to say that all differences can be cleared away neatly by a single counseling session. Another situation we had with an employee didn't go so smoothly. It was especially awkward since this person had been a long-time friend of ours outside of the business and held a top management position in our company at the time.

Bill adopted a new management philosophy and strongly believed in it, so he attempted to implement it throughout the company. We tried for several years to adopt this new approach, but found that parts of it, plus the way it was presented, did not work well for us. These elements were at odds with our own beliefs. This created a management split that was soon reflected in the office as Bill continued to operate his department under his system and the rest of the company operated under ours.

After many counseling sessions, it became clear that our styles were different and a workable compromise was not possible. Bill left the company and now has his own business as a management consultant. I believe if we'd continued to work together, we'd no longer be friends. Our differences would have killed our relationship, and the failed relationship might well have killed the company.

Processes and Games That Give Strength to Relationships

To help people get to know one another better we also often do something called the "Affinity Process." Everyone chooses a partner, preferably someone they know the least, and answers certain questions. The questions we use are:

The Affinity Exercise
   1. *Tell me something I don't know about you;*
   2. *Tell me something you like about me; and*
   3. *Tell me something we have in common.*

One partner asks the other the questions and responds

The "Affinity Process" helps people know each other better and builds support.

Ask your partner these questions, then switch.

Tell me something I don't know about you . . .

::

Tell me something you like about me . . .

::

Tell me something we have in common . . .

only with "Thank you." Then they switch. They repeat the series of questions three times—yes, the same questions three times. People always come up with something new every time and often it's the third round that has the most impact. Then they change partners. This gives everyone a chance to talk to others on a more personal level and plants the seeds of stronger relationships. During this activity, people find they share common interests and often form new friendships. We discovered through this process that we had several singers and musicians in our office, and never knew it. Even staff who have known each other for years usually discover new things about one another.

A Final Word on Relationships

Strong relationships are the basis of strength in a company. For our company, relationships have made all the difference. Building such relationships takes time and effort, but I firmly believe that if you invest in them, you'll receive ten times your investment in return.

Celebrate Your Learning!

❗ *What is the biggest problem in the workplace?*

According to Dr. W. Edwards Deming, it is fear.

❗ *What does "Speak with Good Purpose" mean and why is it important to your life and work?*

It means communicate with positive intent; make it honest and direct. It's important because your words help to determine your thoughts, and the results you achieve in life are directly related to your thoughts.

❗ *What is "Active Listening" and how can it help you?*

Active Listening is the art of listening attentively to someone and letting him know he has been heard. It helps relationships by moving the conversation along and by helping people to understand one another.

❗ *What's the best way to apologize to a customer or co-worker?*

Use the Four-Part Apology:

1. Acknowledge   (take responsibility)
2. Apologize   (state damage you caused)
3. Make It Right   (offer a solution)
4. Recommit   (to appropriate behavior)

4

When Your Mind Meets Your WIIFM

 What does WIIFM mean?

 Why is finding your WIIFM important?

 How does discovering your WIIFM help you adapt to a changing world?

 Why is discovering your WIIFM important to long-term memory and to learning something new?

Y ou are a born "learning machine." You've been learning new skills since the day you came into this world, and you continue to learn something new every day. Not only are you constantly learning, you're constantly adapting to new information and new situations as they come up. Both of these abilities—learning and adapting—are enhanced by how motivated you are, how emotionally "juiced up" you are about a situation. So if you're going to keep pace with the rapidly changing world of business, you must not only use your abilities, you must also repeatedly find the motivation to take action.

Look at your achievements. If you're like most people, you mastered the art of walking when you were about one year old. You stood up, wobbled and fell dozens of times before taking those first steps, but you were motivated. By age two, the desire to discover, interact with and control your environment drove you to learn to communicate through speech. By age five, you had already mastered 90 percent of your adult vocabulary. By age seven you tackled one of the most difficult and complex learning tasks a human being can undertake: you learned to read. Your brain figured out how to associate symbols with sounds, processing them into words in a split second.

During the first years of your life, you were soaking up information and developing skills at an incredible rate. But why? Were you rewarded with a new toy every time you learned a word or mastered a skill? Probably not. What drove you to learn? What motivated you to do so much?

At that age, you were intrinsically motivated to examine every object, explore every new stimulus and take on every new skill—purely to satisfy your hunger to learn. In short, you learned for the sake of learning. At birth, you had burst into the world with your motivation already in place, and you acted on that motivation from the first moment of your life.

Today, you still need to learn new information at an incredible rate if you're going to stay on top of the changes going on around you. Whether it's taking on new assignments as part of expanded responsibilities at work, being forced to learn a new career, or voluntarily start a new business—you need new skills and knowledge to keep things running.

Just keeping up with day-to-day changes in your field can be overwhelming. There are newspapers, trade journals, and reports to read; new work-related technology to master and "new/improved" software programs to be learned or relearned.

Unfortunately, some of us had negative experiences in school and were labeled "poor learners" or "slow learners." Even if you weren't branded as negatively as that, you may still be carrying around ideas about yourself such as "I can't do math; I read slowly; I hate giving speeches." Sometime during elementary school, many of us lost our craving for knowledge. Our activities were being monitored, judged, and graded. We could pass—or we could fail. After a few failures, we learned to take fewer risks, and as we took fewer risks our learning slowed. Fear of failure replaced the yearning to learn.

The trouble is, when you resist learning, you stop growing, and when that happens you put artificial limitations on what you can accomplish in life. To become a Quantum Learner, you need to change your negative beliefs about your ability to learn into a positive, confident recognition that you can learn anything you need or want to. Recapture that motivation that drove you as a young child, and you'll have greater control over your ever-changing world, working and living more effectively.

But how do you recapture your childlike motivation? You're no longer a wide-eyed toddler, driven by a natural hunger to explore a new world. You're an adult with a job and a family and bills to pay, and at the end of the day, probably sore feet and a headache too. What's going to get you excited about learning? The answer is WIIFM (pronounced WHIFF-EM)—an acronym for What's In It For Me. WIIFM is what motivates us to do something; it's the benefit we get from our actions.

Before you do almost anything in your life, you either consciously or subconsciously ask yourself this important question: "What's in it for me?" From the simplest daily task to the monumental life-altering decision, everything has to promise some personal benefit, or you have no motivation to do it. Sometimes the WIIFM is very clear in your mind; other times you have to look for it, or even invent it. Because of the way the human brain works, it's extremely important that you find the WIIFM in every learning situation. And to see why this is so, we need to take a closer look at the miraculous creation called the human brain.

How You Learn: The Mechanics of the Brain

Different parts of your brain control different mental and bodily functions. Since you depend so much on this organ and its parts, it's time you got to know them better.

A journey of discovery through the different parts of your brain is like a trip through human evolution. There is the brain stem, also called the reptilian brain; the limbic system, or mammalian brain; and the neocortex. Together these elements comprise the "triune brain," a term coined by researcher Dr. Paul MacLean.

The reptilian brain, the first area to develop, is at the

WIIFM is what motivates us to do something.

Before you do almost anything
in your life, ask:

WHAT'S IN IT FOR ME?

pg 92

base of your brain and controls the lowest level of your intelligence—primarily survival instincts and sensory motor functions. Your drive to find food and shelter, reproduce, claim and protect territory, and "fight or flee" comes from the reptilian brain. It's called the reptilian brain because all reptiles also develop these basic brain functions.

Next in development is the mammalian brain or limbic system, also called the mid-brain because it sits at the center of your brain. All mammals have this system, which is the seat of emotions, bodily functions, and cognitive thought. It lets you experience feelings—such as love, hate, sorrow, and joy—and controls your metabolism, sleep patterns, hunger and thirst, heart rate, body temperature, and immune system.

It's exciting to know that memory, emotions, and health are all in the same part of your brain—a good reason to keep these three areas of your life in balance. When you're in good emotional and physical health, have strong relationships and communication skills, you're at your peak for learning. When one area is out of balance, it affects how well you learn and perform in the other areas.

The hippocampus, a small part of the forebrain, is the first area to process information, and it plays a crucial role in memory. Larry Squire, Ph.D., a neuropsychologist at the University of California, San Diego, has pioneered a systematic exploration of the components of the brain that process memory and learning. According to Squire, when the hippocampus processes facts and events, it temporarily holds the information, while the brain determines if it's important and valuable. If something is important, the hippocampus helps to store it in specific parts of the neocortex for long-term memory. If the information is not

There are three areas of the brain, together referred to as the "triune brain."

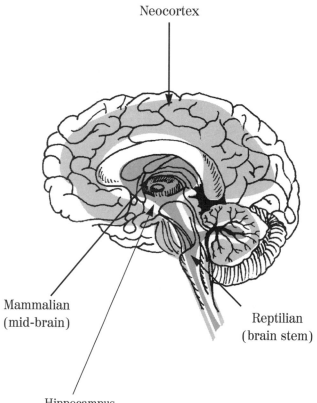

Neocortex

Mammalian
(mid-brain)

Reptilian
(brain stem)

Hippocampus

According to neuropsychologist Larry Squire,
the hippocampus temporarily holds information,
while the brain determines if it's important and
valuable, and then stores it in the neocortex in
long-term memory.

deemed valuable, it may soon be forgotten. This is why it's so important to find the value (the "WIIFM") in things we need to learn, so that information will be stored in the neocortex in long-term memory.

The neocortex marks the final stage of your current brain development. It's an area about the size of a chessboard, a quarter-inch thick, that's been "wrinkled up" to fit in your head. This "gray matter" envelops the lower functioning parts of your brain. The seat of your intellect, the neocortex processes electrical messages. Reasoning, cerebral thinking, decision-making, purposeful behavior and language are found in the neocortex.

The neocortex has left and right hemispheres, with each hemisphere controlling different functions. Although there is crossover, the left hemisphere is primarily logical, sequential, linear, and rational. Its functions are favored by our society and our school system. Language, writing, reading, math, assimilating details and understanding symbolism are left-hemisphere activities.

The right hemisphere is unordered, intuitive, holistic, and random. It's geared toward nonverbal elements like feelings and emotions, spatial awareness, shape and pattern recognition, music, art, color, creativity, and visualization.

You're a more effective learner and business person when you consciously use both sides of your brain. Yet unless you're an artist, musician, or work in some other highly creative position, you probably emphasize left-hemisphere activities in your work. Techniques that more strongly engage both the left and right hemispheres speed up the learning process, increase performance, and improve retention and recall. By including right-hemisphere activities in your heavily left-hemisphere career, you'll learn faster, become more intuitive and creative

Include right-hemisphere activities in your heavily left-hemisphere career to become a more effective learner and business person.

Left	Right
Logical	Emotional
Rational	Intuitive
Sequential	Holistic
Linear	Random/unordered
Detailed	Global/big picture
Language	Music
Writing	Spatial awareness
Reading	Creating
Math	Art

when solving problems, and may even experience sudden flashes of insight in your work.

Quantum Learning employs what are thought of as both left- and right-hemisphere activities, which make learning easier and more rewarding. So as you get caught up in a cycle of continuous growth and improvement, you want to learn more.

- The more you learn, the more you understand.
- The more you understand, the better your business and career decisions will be.
- The better your decisions, the more successful you become.
- The more successful you are, the more fun and fulfillment you find in learning . . . and the cycle begins again.

The truth is, we all share the same neurology, stretching back to such famous thinkers as Leonardo da Vinci and Albert Einstein. There are an estimated 100 billion nerve cells in our brains, each with axons and dendrites that connect more strongly with one another when we learn something new. The number of possible connections is— well, mind-boggling. Biologically speaking, we each have the potential to become a genius. In reality, we develop the parts of our brains that we need. When we believe we need to learn something for our survival or interest, we learn it. When we discover benefits for knowing something, we make the effort to know it. Our capacity for learning new things is, for all practical purposes, limitless. So our knowledge and intelligence will increase by our perceived need to know. Developing a strong desire to do something and perceiving it as a real need is what I call "finding our WIIFM."

How you feel about yourself spills over into everything

you do. When you leave behind the attitude that you can't learn, and discover powerful reasons why you must learn, you'll find you're empowered with the ability to achieve all you want in life.

At Learning Forum, people who work with us are drawn by the vision and the work we do with youth. The WIIFMs are often the good feelings we get when we observe the enthusiasm and excitement of students at our programs. The WIIFMs are the letters from graduates and their parents telling us of the positive changes in their lives.

After the first SuperCamp, I was "hooked." I knew that youth programs were where I wanted to focus my energies. I look forward to going into the office and working on projects that interest me. I love having a feeling of purpose, and I enjoy working with people I like and respect. These things make for strong WIIFMs.

What can you do if there are no apparent WIIFMs in place in your situation? First, it's important to look at what's really in it for you in your job or business. Are you doing something you don't like simply for the security, the money, or the investment you've made in being an expert in that area? If so, it may look as if you have no WIIFMs in your job. Yet security can be a strong motivator. Being able to sleep at night is most certainly a WIIFM. However, if security is your only WIIFM, you may be paying too high a price for it. To sacrifice challenge, excitement, joy, and adventure for security—well, that you'll have to decide for yourself. To me, it's giving security more importance than it deserves.

Every day I have to think about what it means to own a business. The WIIFMs are enormous: personal satisfaction, constant newness, freedom, financial rewards. But all of these have an opposite side as well. There's worry, huge liability, unexpected upsets, and the possibility of losing everything. It's important for each person to thoughtfully look at what it is they want. For some, the grass always looks greener in some other field or situation. If that's you, recognize it about yourself. Then try to look openly at the positives and negatives of your situation, and weigh the WIIFMs for yourself. Focusing on the WIIFMs means taking responsibility for your choices.

When you search for your WIIFM, you may find it's related to your vision. It may be a small part of reaching your vision, like making calls quickly to improve customer service, which in turn helps you realize your goal of helping your company become a model of excellence in customer relations. Or it could be the vision itself that motivates you. Either way, you're thinking long-term and becoming intrinsically motivated, and thus are more likely to stick with your goals and find satisfaction in your achievements.

Remember to ask yourself "What's In It for Me?"—and you'll discover how a strong motive can unleash the power of your mind.

Celebrate Your Learning!

! *What does WIIFM mean?*

WIIFM is an acronym for "What's In It For Me." Finding your WIIFM helps you discover your motivation.

! *Why is finding your WIIFM important?*

Finding your WIIFM helps you become intrinsically motivated, increasing your chances to stay with a project and succeed. When you're intrinsically motivated, projects become personally rewarding, interesting, and joyful.

! *How does discovering your WIIFM help you adapt to a changing world?*

To keep up with change, you need to learn new information at an incredible rate. Discovering your WIIFM can help you change negative beliefs about learning into positive affirmations of your amazing ability to learn.

! *Why is discovering your WIIFM important to long-term memory and to learning something new?*

The hippocampus temporarily holds new information, deciding whether it's valuable, then sends it to the neocortex where it's stored in long-term memory. A strong WIIFM increases the likelihood information will be stored in long-term memory.

5

Integrity Paves the Way to Achievement

 What two elements define integrity?

 What effect does living in integrity have on your life?

 What are the steps to greater integrity?

 What is the essence of integrity?

H ave you ever heard the expression "Walk your talk"? It means, don't just tell us your values or ideals; demonstrate them in your actions. Live them and be them. That's integrity.

When your behavior matches your values, you have integrity. By values, I mean your business principles, personal values, and vision. When your behavior and values are aligned, you feel good about what you're doing. Your self-esteem rises and so does your success rate. But when your actions conflict with your values, you're more likely to get a nagging feeling that what you're doing isn't right, even if it's helping you reach a goal.

Some examples in which values and behavior don't match might be:

- Valuing honesty, yet cheating on your income taxes.
- Telling employees to always be on time, but being late yourself.
- Expecting others to stick to a budget, then exceeding your own budget.
- Wanting a successful business, but refusing to learn the financial side of it.
- Valuing keeping your word and promising to meet a deadline, then procrastinating and missing it.

Note: If you don't value keeping your word and don't keep it, you may be perceived as unreliable and even unethical, but you're not lacking integrity. You have integrity when your actions match your values.

There's a concept in geometry that explains integrity very well: congruence. When one shape exactly fits over another, they are congruent. They are identical in size and shape. When our behavior and our values are congruent, we're living with integrity.

You are in integrity when your behavior matches your values.

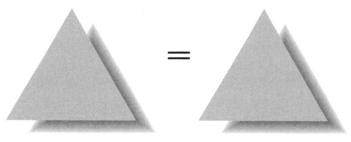

Behavior   **Values**

Congruent Triangles

*When your behavior and values are aligned,
they are congruent—you are in integrity.*

Integrity—What's in It for Me?

Why do we need integrity? If we find a way to save a little on taxes, why not cheat? Who will know, or care?

Living with integrity can be challenging. Often, there appears to be a greater benefit in disregarding values than in keeping them. Many of us find it easy to justify: "Taxes are too high." "I paid too much last year." "The government owes me," and so on. A clear conscience may not seem like much compared to $500 saved. However, disregarding values, for whatever reason, usually results in repercussions of some kind . . . eventually. For example, sweating through an IRS audit, and then having to pay the $500 you thought you'd saved plus several hundred more in penalties. Or being late on a project and then finding your employees or peers are also late. (They probably thought "It must be okay if my boss and others are doing it.")

Sticking with your values, on the other hand, has important long-term payoffs. In my own life, I find that when I live with integrity, I build trust. Others know that I'll keep my word, and they can depend on me. As my reputation grows, so does my influence. Because I'm trusted, more people want to work for me, do business with me, and buy my products. I gain the trust and respect of my colleagues, customers, family, and friends.

I find living with integrity is often a matter of choosing between short-term and long-term benefits. When I invested in stock options, the short-term benefits were enormous, and although we were risking money that could have been spent on the business, I found ways to justify what I was doing. I had the best intentions: we were working toward our goal of building up the Burklyn Business School, and the school, students, and investors would all profit. It seemed like an immediate path to success.

But what we were doing was shortsighted and out of integrity. I believe in win/win, and I knew deep down that in stock options, in order for one person to win, another has to lose. I was taking a chance. Eventually I was the loser, and it all came crashing down.

Discovering Values

The stock option crisis spurred me to examine my actions and my values. It showed me where they were incongruent. We can all learn from each other's mistakes. Learn from mine, and take time now to become aware of your values. This is the first step to greater integrity.

One way to do this is to look at the values you admire in your friends. Do you appreciate them for their honesty, compassion, or generosity? Do you cultivate these qualities in yourself? Look at areas of your life that are important to you, such as family, friendships, community service, or your career. How do your values show up in these areas? Are you in integrity, or do your actions conflict with your values? Take time to reflect on these questions.

Living with integrity takes a high level of self-awareness. You really have to know yourself and your values. Based on that knowledge, you formulate your vision and develop your goals. This means you'll have to "check in" with yourself when you find you're justifying an action. Pause and examine why you're doing it. If the thing you're justifying, is incongruent with your values, stop it—period.

Integrity in Action

Integrity is an expression of who you are. If you're an honest person, you'll be truthful in your business dealings and your relationships. If you value keeping your word, you'll do your best to always follow through. You'll follow your values regardless of circumstances. Let's say you're offered $20 to falsely testify against someone in court. You refuse because you value honesty. Later, the offer is increased to $2,000, then $200,000. Is there a point where the circumstances become more important to you than your values? When you're operating out of integrity, you stick to your values regardless of circumstances. If you value something, you should be willing to stick with it.

Integrity also means doing what you expect others to do. As a personal policy, I participate in all the events and courses we ask the students to do at SuperCamp. When we add a new event to our outdoor challenge course, I try it out. When we add a new element to our curriculum, I learn it. Whether it's jumping off a 30-foot pole to catch a trapeze or practicing the new speed-reading technique, if we expect the students to do it, then I do it too.

This principle applies to any business. Live up to the expectations you set for others, and they'll be more likely to follow. If you tell your employees to always maintain a professional image, then coming to work in your exercise clothes is incongruent. If you run a nonsmoking office, you're out of integrity if you're always running outside for a cigarette. Be willing to do the things you expect others to do. Set the example.

Maintaining Integrity

To fulfill your dreams, your actions must be congruent with your goals. Most successful people have clearly written goals and vision statements. They plan the action steps needed to achieve those goals. Commitment to your vision can keep you on course when you're being pulled in too many directions. A tool that can serve as your road map to greater integrity and success is Outcome Thinking.

Integrity is an expression of who you are.

If you value:

Honesty — be truthful

**Keeping
your word** — follow through

Being fair — do what you expect
others to do

Outcome Thinking

For this exercise, you'll need some paper, a pen, a quiet place to think, and the willingness to do some soul-searching. Take time to think about these questions in depth. Some may be quite clear to you; others could challenge you to examine your current lifestyle and direction more closely.

- What do I value about my life, my health, my career, my family, my friends?

- Am I doing activities that support these values?

- What inspires me? What do I want my life to be about?

Decide where you want to be in one year, five years, and ten years. Write out a detailed scenario for each, including career, personal relationships, finances, health, and education. Describe in detail what your life will be like at that time. Think about where you'd like to live, whether you're married or single, have children, where you are in your career, where you take your vacations, whatever is important to you. Don't censure your ideas as too wild or impractical; dream big. Once you clearly formulate your goals and set a point of focus in your life, you'll begin to tune in on the opportunities around you and bring your dream to fruition.

Picture your vision—your idealistic, inspiring picture of what could be, the force that drives you forward. Think about some goals that can move you toward that vision. What action steps are you taking to reach those goals? Again, writing it down and picturing it in your mind helps make it happen. A clear vision gives you direction. Goals help you formulate the steps to get you there.

Integrity is more than good actions.

Values   **Behavior**

*Integrity is a heartfelt belief in your values and
a true desire to uphold them.*

Living with integrity gives you power. It raises your self-respect and earns you the trust and respect of others. When you live with integrity regarding your values and vision, you're more likely to find success—not only in business, but in every aspect of your life.

Celebrate Your Learning!

! *What two elements define integrity?*

Values and behavior. When they're aligned, you're in integrity.

! *What effect does living in integrity have on your life?*

When you're in integrity, you feel better about what you're doing, your self-esteem rises, and your success rate goes up.

! *What are the steps to greater integrity?*

First, becoming aware of your values, goals, and vision. Next, becoming aware of your behavior.

! *What is the essence of integrity?*

Congruence; having your activities and behavior congruent with your desired outcomes and values.

6

Getting the Most from Your Personality and Learning Style

 Why is it important to know that people learn in different ways?

 How can you categorize people when each person is an individual?

 In taking learning styles tests, what influences your choices?

 Do different models measure the same thing?

H ave you ever given what you thought were perfectly clear instructions for a project or procedure to a co-worker, only to find he didn't seem to understand a word you said? Or maybe you've been on the other side of miscommunication, frustrated and lost in a fog of misunderstanding, wondering how you became so dense all of a sudden.

With some people, you never seem able to get your point across. You feel as if you're talking to a statue. On the other hand, you probably have some friends who always understand you; they seem to get what you mean almost before you say it. Why is communication so easy with some people and so difficult with others?

Everyone Learns in Different Ways

The answer is so obvious, it's almost a cliché, yet it may surprise you. As you know, each person is different, with unique abilities and gifts. What you may not know, (or may not have thought about), is that each individual also learns in different ways. Thus the manner in which we're taught or spoken to greatly affects what we learn. The key to clear communication and greater learning ability is understanding not only your own learning style, but also the learning styles of others. By knowing how you learn best and by recognizing how others learn, you can discover how to pick up knowledge more easily and communicate more effectively.

The term "learning styles" applies to anything that affects how we learn. This includes the way we take in and process information, plus the ways we think and communicate. Researchers from a number of fields have come up with their own models for identifying different types of learners. Although the names and terminology may vary, most learning style models are surprisingly similar and many find their roots in the theories of the legendary psychiatrist, Carl Jung.

Research shows that understanding greatly increases when you match your activities with your strongest learning style. According to Rita Dunn, a professor at John Hopkins University, students taught in their preferred learning style have improved attitudes toward learning, increased tolerance for different ways of learning, and increased academic achievement. One of the major benefits of discovering your learning style is that it allows you to take "ownership" of your learning. You can use it to get the most out of seminars, workshops, courses, and the everyday material you must assimilate.

Improving Communication with Style

You can improve communication (and results), when you know how to recognize and tap in to the best learning styles of other people. This information will help you improve rapport with your co-workers, clients, and spouse; become a better negotiator; make more sales; enrich your relationships; increase your successes. All this happens because understanding learning styles helps you know yourself and others. It helps you recognize the best, most effective ways to reach all types of people.

In this chapter, we'll explore several different learning style models. Each one identifies different types of learners and describes some of their habits and abilities. As you read, please keep in mind that these are useful generalizations and do not perfectly describe any one person all the time. Use the categories and labels as guidelines, and remember that people change with their circumstances, sometimes favoring one or another learning strategy.

Psycho-Geometric Personality Styles

Take a look at the shapes on the right-hand page. Think of each shape as a person, and in the space provided, write three adjectives that best describe the shape to you. For example, you might describe the Circle as "well-rounded."

Do this now.

Next, choose the shape you feel is most like you—the one that best represents you—and rank it number one. Then rank your next-favorite shape number two, and so on, until you have ranked them all, one through five. Your number-one shape is your primary shape.

Take time now to complete this exercise so you can get the most out of this chapter.

You've just taken the Psycho-Geometrics personality indicator test, developed by Susan Dellinger, Ph.D. This simple test can tell you a great deal about how your brain works. According to Dr. Dellinger, author of *Psycho-Geometrics, How to Use Geometric Psychology to Influence People* (Prentice-Hall, Englewood Cliffs, New Jersey, 1989), your personality, experience, education, and the way your brain functions all combine to draw you toward certain shapes. The choices you make and how you perceive the world have a lot to do with whether you favor the left or right hemisphere of your brain.

As mentioned in Chapter 4, the left and right hemispheres of the brain process information differently. The left hemisphere is logical, sequential, linear, and rational. The right is unordered, intuitive, holistic, and random. Although there is crossover, your dominant hemisphere determines how you think.

Left-hemisphere thinkers do best in activities that are

Who are you?

Directions:

- Write 3 adjectives that best describe the shapes.
- Choose your favorite (#1).
- Rank the others (#2–#5).

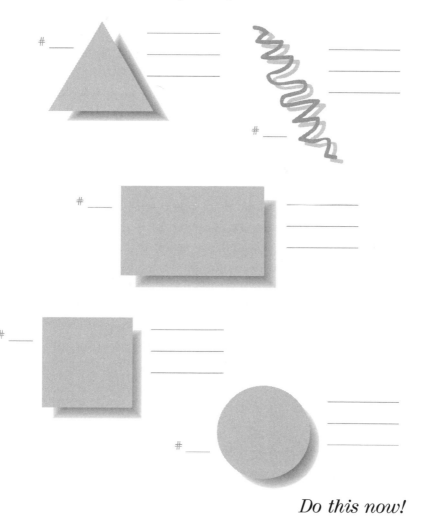

Do this now!

logical and sequential, and they usually choose the linear shapes. They're more likely to be in a highly structured job such as accountant, secretary, or administrator.

Right-hemisphere thinkers tend to be more creative and intuitive, and usually choose the Circle or Squiggle as representing them best. They may pursue careers in the arts, or the "helping professions" such as nursing or psychology. Now, let's take a look at your test results.

What Shape Are You?

Your number-one shape is an indicator of how you think and behave. Read the description of the shape you chose. Does this person sound familiar? You probably won't match all the attributes of your shape perfectly, but it should paint a pretty good picture of who you are and the ways you learn and communicate.

Triangle Characteristics

Triangles are well-balanced, and their focus is at the top—on goals, career, and moving forward. They have strong leadership skills and are quick to make decisions and take action. They're often athletic and love to compete. Political maneuvering is a strong point with them, and they have the ability to empower others. They're sometimes described as role models.

Other Triangle traits include a driving need to be in control and to be seen as "right." These types are often more interested in their careers than in the work itself, and although they're quick decision-makers, they're likely to choose the course that's in their best interest. They would rather be the team leader than the team player.

Communicating with Triangles

Since Triangles are quick decision-makers and left-hemisphere thinkers, you need to present information to them quickly, clearly, and succinctly. Make sure you have researched all the facts ahead of time. Triangles like information presented logically and sequentially, so avoid jumping around from topic to topic. They like to get to the point quickly.

Triangles often lose emotional control in an argument, so if you can keep your cool you'll have the advantage. If you know you'll be facing an emotional situation with a Triangle, you may want to practice the conversation with a friend ahead of time.

Box Characteristics

The Box is the most structured shape. Box types are hardworking, dedicated, persistent—the ones who get the job done. They're detail-oriented and highly organized. They love factual data, and dislike emotional issues. They're happiest when their lives are controlled and predictable. Following directions and completing projects are their strong points. They're weaker at developing their own plans. Tell them what to do, and they do it.

Boxes are not strong decision-makers. When unsure of what course to take, they often put off making any decision at all, until forced to do so. They often resist change until they have all the facts and evidence supporting a need for change, and even then may prefer the status quo. They have trouble functioning in an unstructured, disorganized environment. Their highly developed analytical side makes them appear cool and aloof, and their love of details can lead them to be nit-picking perfectionists.

Communicating with Boxes

Boxes hate conflict and usually try to avoid it. They're uncomfortable expressing emotion and prefer to solve problems logically and analytically. Boxes will collaborate with others to solve problems as long as the situation remains unemotional and there's plenty of factual data to go on.

When you have to make a proposal to a Box, do your homework. Boxes like to get all the facts, and they'll be armed with their own detailed information. They also prefer to see things in writing and they like reports.

Circle Characteristics

Circles are amiable, caring, even-tempered, and well-rounded. They're social "people persons." Family and friends are important to them. They want to please others and they strive to make sure everyone is happy. They're definitely team players who dislike conflict and will extend themselves to make things right.

Good interpersonal relations are important to Circles. Their natural empathy, genuine caring, and ability to listen make them the best communicators.

On the downside, Circles sometimes try too hard to please and have trouble saying "no." Others sometimes take advantage of them or manipulate them. They don't like making unpopular decisions or causing upset or strife. At times they spend so much time and energy on others that they neglect their own needs. They also tend to blame themselves when things go wrong.

Communicating with Circles

A Circle with a problem likes to talk about his feelings and can monopolize your time if you let him. Be careful not to encourage this behavior.

In conflicts, work for a win/win outcome. Demonstrate how the solution will please others. Help the Circle focus on the problem at hand, rather than on emotions and rela-

Personality Style Characteristics

- Strong leadership skills
- Quick decision-makers
- Athletic
- Ability to empower others
- Need to control
- Left-hemisphere thinkers

- Idea generators
- Conceptualizers
- Focused on future
- Expressive
- Motivators
- Unstructured
- Right-hemisphere thinkers

- Undergoing change
- Searching for something new
- Learning and growing
- Open to new ideas
- Unpredictable

- Detail-oriented
- Highly organized
- Love factual data
- Follow directions
- Complete projects
- Resist making decisions
- Left-hemisphere thinkers

- Social "people persons"
- Pleasers
- Team players
- Strong interpersonal skills
- Good communication
- Right-hemisphere thinkers

tionships, and make it clear that the discussion will be kept confidential. Be prepared to deal with hurt feelings. When working with a Circle, help him prioritize his work. Give him a deadline.

Squiggle Characteristics

The Squiggle shape symbolizes creativity. Squiggles are the creative, intuitive, right-hemisphere thinkers. They're likely to experience leaps in thinking, jumping to conclusions or getting a sudden inspiration. Ideas and the big picture interest them more than details. They get excited about new concepts and like to focus on the future. They're naturally expressive and able to motivate others.

However, Squiggles can be disorganized and forgetful of details. Also, they can be difficult for others to understand and their leaps in thought and unstructured manner can frustrate the more structured shapes. The Squiggle doesn't function well in a highly structured environment.

Communicating with Squiggles

Squiggles are powerful, persuasive speakers and often win arguments. However, if you patiently listen to the Squiggle's side first, the Squiggle will be more likely to listen to you. Try to express as much enthusiasm for your ideas as the Squiggle shows for his.

The Squiggle's right-brain leaps in thinking can be difficult for more sequential thinkers to follow, and Squiggles get upset when they're misunderstood. Ask questions and rephrase what the Squiggle has just said to make sure you understand. The Squiggle will feel better knowing you truly do want to understand him and take him seriously.

Rectangle Characteristics

Rectangles represent transition. They're in a temporary state—undergoing major changes in life, questioning their

Typical Jobs

- executive
- manager/supervisor
- entrepreneur
- hospital/school administrator
- politician
- law firm partner
- union organizer
- military officer

- strategic planner
- artist/performer/poet
- university professor
- international sales
- inventor
- musician
- promoter/
  public relations agent

- new bosses
- new graduates
- entrepreneurs
- entry level employees
- performers
- people in midife crisis
- new retirees

- accountant
- administrator
- administrative assistant
- doctor
- teacher
- computer programmer
- government worker
- bank teller

- teacher/trainer
- nurse/doctor
- salesperson
- secretary
- mental health professional
- human resources
- camp counselor

current situation or searching for something new. Rectangles are learning and growing and are excited about upcoming changes in their lives. They're open to new ideas and experiences, but are also easily swayed by any new fad that comes along. They're confused and inconsistent, with personalities that seem to change from day to day, making them very unpredictable. Plus, they're not above some emotional outbursts.

Communicating with Rectangles

A Rectangle may change his mind often. He has trouble reaching a decision, and because he's unsure, you're likely to win him over if you present your information clearly, confidently, and convincingly. Find a win/win solution, and finalize everything by putting it in writing. Also, because Rectangles are so unsteady, be sure to offer them lots of support and encouragement.

The Psycho-Geometrics test gives you a good overall picture of how you learn, communicate, and handle the everyday situations that come up in your life. There are, however, many more tests to measure the way you learn.

The Gregorc Model of Brain Dominance

Anthony Gregorc, professor of curriculum and instruction at the University of Connecticut, has developed a model of brain dominance: the way our brains best process information. His categories are similar to the left-hemisphere/right-hemisphere dominance we mentioned earlier. Gregorc identifies two main ways we process information: concrete and abstract perception; and sequential and random perception.

He combines these two ways of thinking to form four distinct categories: concrete sequential, abstract sequen-

Read each set of words and mark the two that best describe you:

1. a. imaginative
   b. investigative
   c. realistic
   d. analytical

2. a. organized
   b. adaptable
   c. rational
   d. inquisitive

3. a. debating
   b. getting to the point
   c. creating
   d. relating to others

4. a. empathetic
   b. practical
   c. academic
   d. adventurous

5. a. precise
   b. flexible
   c. systematic
   d. inventive

6. a. sharing
   b. orderly
   c. sensible
   d. independent

7. a. competitive
   b. perfectionist
   c. cooperative
   d. logical

8. a. intellectual
   b. sensitive
   c. hardworking
   d. risk-taking

9. a. nonfiction reader
   b. people person
   c. problem-solver
   d. planner

10. a. memorize
    b. associate
    c. think through
    d. originate

11. a. changer
    b. researcher
    c. spontaneous
    d. wants directions

12. a. communicating
    b. discovering
    c. cautious
    d. reasoning

13. a. challenging
    b. practicing
    c. caring
    d. examining

14. a. completing work
    b. seeing possibilities
    c. gaining ideas
    d. interpreting

15. a. doing
    b. feeling
    c. thinking
    d. experimenting

tial, concrete random, and abstract random. The sequential thinkers are generally left-hemisphere-dominant, and the random thinkers rely more heavily on the right hemisphere. As with Psycho-Geometrics, knowing what type of thinker you are can help you make the most of your learning abilities and can improve your communication with others whose brains may work differently from yours.

The test on the previous page was designed by John Parks Le Tellier, an educational consultant and SuperCamp instructor. This test helps you determine how you process information. After you take the test, check your results by marking answers on the columns on the right-hand page.

Concrete Sequential

These types of thinkers process information in an ordered, step-by-step fashion. Their world is physical and concrete; it consists of the things they can see, touch, hear, taste, and smell. Concrete sequential thinkers are detail-oriented and can remember facts, data, and formulas easily. They learn best by doing. They're organizers and perfectionists.

Concrete Random

Like concrete sequentials, concrete random thinkers live in the concrete, physical world. However, their behavior is less structured and they like to experiment. They're often more creative and experience intuitive leaps in thought when searching for a solution. When working on a project, they often get more caught up in the process than in the final outcome, and may lose track of time and miss deadlines. They love to look for alternative ways of doing things and explore new ideas or systems. They follow divergent thought processes.

QUANTUM BUSINESS

Directions:

- In the columns below, circle the two letters you chose for each number.
- Add totals for columns I, II, III, and IV.
- Multiply the total of each column by 4.
- The box with the highest number describes how you most often process information.

	I	II	III	IV
1.	C	D	A	B
2.	A	C	B	D
3.	B	A	D	C
4.	B	C	A	D
5.	A	C	B	D
6.	B	C	A	D
7.	B	D	C	A
8.	C	A	B	D
9.	D	A	B	C
10.	A	C	B	D
11.	D	B	C	A
12.	C	D	A	B
13.	B	D	C	A
14.	A	C	D	B
15.	A	C	B	D
	Total	Total	Total	Total
	___	___	___	___

I.   ____ x 4 = [   ] Concrete Sequential (CS)

II. ____ x 4 = [   ] Abstract Sequential (AS)

III. ____ x 4 = [   ] Abstract Random   (AR)

IV. ____ x 4 = [   ] Concrete Random   (CR)

Abstract Random

Feelings and emotions are primary parts of the abstract random thinkers' world. They need time to reflect on new information before making a decision or forming an opinion. They remember best when information is personalized, and like to see the whole picture before getting into the details to get a clear understanding. They dislike structured environments and are people oriented. They do well in positions where they can use their creativity.

Abstract Sequential

Abstract sequential thinkers live in a world of theory and thought. They like to analyze information and think in concepts. Their thinking processes are logical, rational, and intellectual, and they like well-organized information and events. Abstract sequential thinkers do well at research, as they are avid readers and find it easy to pinpoint key ideas and information. They're inquisitive and want to understand theories and causes behind effects.

Gregorc's four categories reveal strategies for making learning easy and natural. Take a close look at the descriptions and think of ways you can apply this information to enhance your learning. If you're an abstract random thinker, for example, you may want to get general overviews of new projects or data, then find out how that fits into the bigger picture and how it's valuable to you. Doing this will give the information context and meaning, making it easier for you to delve into the details.

You may have also noticed some similarities between Gregorc's models and Psycho-Geometrics. For example there are some Box characteristics in the concrete sequen-

Model of Brain Dominance

Chart your learning style by marking your
scores on the grid below:

Left Hemisphere   Right Hemisphere

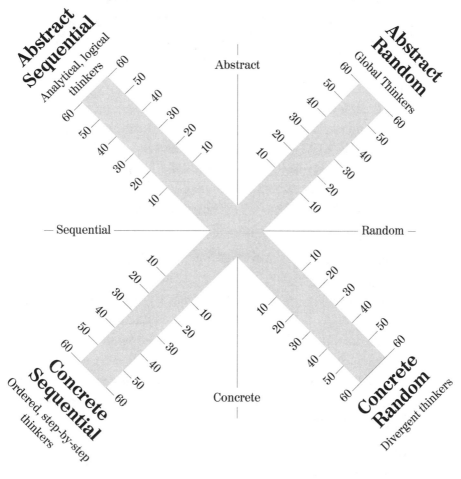

tial thinker—logical, organized, detail-oriented—while the concrete random's people-oriented style is reminiscent of the friendly Circle.

VAK: Seeing, Hearing, Feeling

VAK stands for Visual, Auditory, and Kinesthetic. This is one of the most commonly used tools for evaluating the way people learn, and is cropping up in schools across the country. VAK measures the way we take in information and is built around our senses—what we see, hear, and feel. We use all three of these senses to learn, but we usually favor one. Here's a breakdown:

Visual

These learners need to see information, either in writing or in charts, graphs, pictures, or other visual aids. They can remember what was seen and they will visually reproduce it. Visuals need a big picture and purpose. They use expressions like: "picture this . . ." "looks like . . ." "see . . . " and "focus here . . ."

Auditory

As you can guess, listening and vocalizing are the keys for these types of learners. They learn as if they have a tape recorder in their head, retrieving information exactly as they heard it. They can also mimic tone and pitch. They learn well in lectures and by repeating information and talking to themselves. You'll hear an auditory use these expressions: "sounds like . . ." "rings a bell . . ." "listen . . ." "I hear you loud and clear . . ."

Kinesthetic/Tactile

Hands-on learning works best for kinesthetics. They learn through experience and actions. They remember

VAK measures the way we take in information.

 Visual learners need to see information

 Auditory learners need to hear and vocalize information

 Kinesthetic / Tactile learners need to have experiences and are referred to as "hands-on" learners feelings and an overall impression of the information. They say things like: "grasp the concept," "get a handle on it," "I'm touched," and "slipped my mind." Tactile learners like to physically manipulate objects in order to grasp the information.

You may already recognize yourself in one of these descriptions. Recognizing preferred learning styles makes it easier for trainers to reach their students. Plus, it greatly enhances communication and employee relations. But VAK doesn't stop here. Dawna Markova, learning styles specialist and co-author of *How Your Child Is Smart* (Conari Press, Berkeley, Calif. 1992), takes VAK one step further. She stresses that we use all three methods, visual, auditory and kinesthetic, but in different sequences, which in turn correspond to our three different states of mind. She calls these sequences "personal thinking patterns."

Thinking Patterns

Our personal thinking pattern reflects the way we take information in, store it in our brains, recall it later, and eventually express it. When we learn, information goes first through our conscious mind, then our subconscious, and finally our unconscious mind. According to Markova, we learn best when new information follows this path.

In the conscious state, we organize and evaluate new information. We're alert and focused. The subconscious is the state where we consider information, questioning it, and seeing how it fits with previous learning. In this state we move back and forth from alert to dazed. The unconscious state is where everything sinks in; information is integrated with prior learning, we see the whole situation, and make connections with past experiences. In this state, we experiment and get creative, arranging and rearranging the information in different sequences. We're usually dazed and quiet in this state of mind.

Markova calls VAK the "perceptual channels" that the brain uses to process information, with each channel corresponding to a state. For one person, visual input accesses the conscious state, auditory the subconscious, and kinesthetic the unconscious. However, another learner may do it the other way around, being kinesthetic in the conscious state, auditory in the subconscious, and visual in the unconscious state. There are six different possible combinations—meaning six different ways people learn. We learn best when information is taught in a way that matches our personal thinking pattern.

Identifying Your Thinking Pattern

AKV (Auditory, Kinesthetic, Visual)
"Leaders of the Pack"
These learners are high-energy, take-charge leaders. They express themselves well. They love to debate, tell jokes, or make plays on words. They can remember what was said word for word. They make sounds constantly, either talking to themselves, whistling, humming, or singing. They generally do well in sports and physical activities.

AVK (Auditory, Visual, Kinesthetic)
"Verbal Gymnasts"
AVKs are great talkers, and their verbal ability makes them appear to be very intelligent. Like AKVs, they enjoy debating, storytelling, puns and other verbal feats. They also find it easy to learn new languages. These learners do well in academics but find physical tasks and sports difficult to

master. They may shy away from physical contact and have trouble expressing their emotions.

K/TAV (Kinesthetic/Tactile, Auditory, Visual)
"Movers and Groovers"
K/TAVs are physically oriented; they seem to always be moving (kinesthetic) and like to manipulate objects (tactile). Even when they're supposed to be sitting still, they're tapping their feet or fidgeting. They explore the world through touching, doing, and experiencing. Athletics come naturally to them. They're affectionate and respond to touch. They have trouble focusing on visual material.

KVA (Kinesthetic, Visual, Auditory)
"Wandering Wonderers"
These learners also find it easy to perform physical tasks and sports, are well coordinated, and have a strong, quiet presence. They have a lot of energy and like to keep moving. They keep to themselves and learn by silently observing others' actions. They may have difficulty verbalizing their feelings and may be overwhelmed by too much talk. They like to look at the big picture and recognize how everything fits together.

VKA (Visual, Kinesthetic, Auditory)
"Seers and Feelers"
Seeing and experiencing facilitate learning in VKAs. They easily remember what they have seen or read, and can also learn by imitating someone else's actions. But they may find verbal directions hard to follow. They do their best work in a well-organized environment; they have trouble thinking

Knowing your learning sequence is as important as knowing your preferred way of processing information.

AKV – "Leaders of the Pack"

AVK – "Verbal Gymnasts"

K/TAV – "Movers and Groovers"

KVA – "Wandering Wonderers"

VKA – "Seers and Feelers"

VAK – "Show and Tellers"

clearly when their desk is messy. When speaking, they may have difficulty making themselves understood and it can take them a long time to get to the point.

VAK (Visual, Auditory, Kinesthetic)
"Show and Tellers"
VAKs are social, talkative, and friendly. They learn through visual aids like charts, graphs, and pictures, but also do well listening to lectures and can follow spoken directions. They are avid readers, and find it easy to memorize what they read through note-taking and talking to themselves. They may avoid sports and find it hard to learn physical tasks, such as riding a bike; they need lots of practice to master these kinds of activities. They are uncomfortable being touched.

Knowing the sequence of how you learn is as important as knowing your preferred way of processing information. When new information is presented in a way that accesses your conscious state, you'll learn quickly and stay active and alert. If you're VKA, a chart showing company profits will be easy for you to understand, since your conscious state is visual. If, however, someone tells you about the company profits, your mind may become vacant and you may stare into space, since your unconscious state is hooked up with auditory stimulation. Markova's theory goes a long way toward explaining why some people excel in certain classes while others fall behind. It all has to do with matching learning styles.

Where Do You Fit In? / Putting It All Together

There are many similarities among the three methods of

Personal thinking patterns reflect how we take in information, store it, recall it, and express it.

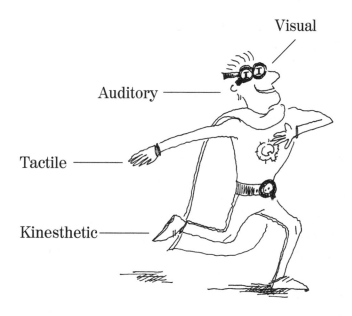

measuring your learning style we just reviewed. The chart on the right-hand page shows how each style relates to the others.

Circle: right-brain dominant
           concrete random
           VKA/VAK

Squiggle: right-brain dominant
           abstract random
           KVA

Triangle: left-brain dominant
           abstract sequential
           AKV, K/TAV

Box: left-brain dominant
           concrete sequential
           AVK

Rectangle: in transition
           May have many different styles and may
           change from day to day.

Some people are mostly one style; that is, nearly all their preferred learning styles are in the same quadrant on the chart. Others may have one strong style with a tendency toward another style. Still others may be spread out all over the chart. These are usually Rectangles!

Whatever your style, the more you know about how you learn, the easier learning can be. Many more methods have been devised for measuring your learning style, personality, behavioral patterns, and so on. The Personal Profile System, sometimes called DISC, is available through Performax Systems International. It's used by many companies to reveal employees' work styles and improve interoffice relations.

There are many similarities among the methods of measuring learning styles.

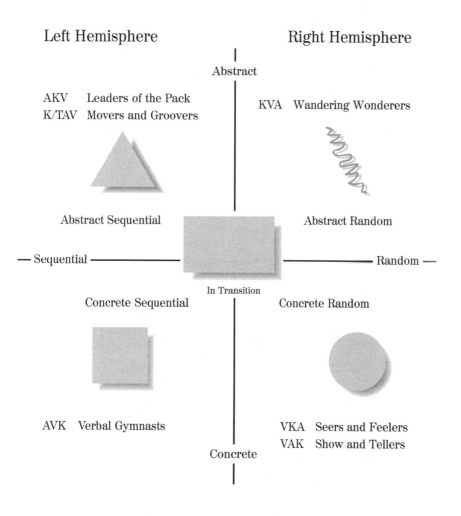

Left Hemisphere

Right Hemisphere

Abstract

AKV   Leaders of the Pack
K/TAV Movers and Groovers

KVA   Wandering Wonderers

Abstract Sequential

Abstract Random

— Sequential ——

—— Random —

In Transition

Concrete Sequential

Concrete Random

AVK   Verbal Gymnasts

VKA   Seers and Feelers
VAK   Show and Tellers

Concrete

The Team Player Survey, developed by Glenn Parker at Jossey-Bass, Inc., also focuses on working styles with an emphasis on group dynamics. This instrument identifies four ways people participate in a team: as Contributor, Collaborator, Communicator or Challenger. The Contributor is task-oriented and organized. The Collaborator is goal-directed and sees the big picture. The Communicator's strengths lie in facilitation, and the Challenger questions everything: methods, processes, and goals. Recognizing the strengths and weaknesses of each type and knowing how they interact helps employees work out their differences.

To know more about your individual preferences for the work environment, you may want to take the Learning Styles Inventory and Productivity Environmental Preference Survey, developed by researchers Rita and Kenneth Dunn. Often referred to as the Dunn & Dunn Test, this method helps you design your optimum work environment. It will help you decide such things as:

- Do you need quiet background music or no music?
- Do you do better with dim or bright light?
- Are you better off working with a partner or alone?
- How much structure do you need?
- What is your most productive time of day?

Think about these aspects as you go through your day and be aware of what works best for you. You can accomplish far more when your environment supports your learning style.

Congratulations! You're now equipped with tools for better understanding yourself and others. Not only do you know how you best learn and communicate, but you can

Identifying your learning styles leads to better understanding of yourself and improved communication with others.

Are you:

❏ Mostly one style?

❏ Strong in one style with tendencies toward others?

❏ Nearly equal in all styles?

recognize the pattern in which you do it. You've also learned strategies for improving your communication with others, and gained some understanding of why you and your co-workers may not always see eye-to-eye. When you need to learn new material in optimum time, remember to use your strengths—your strongest learning style. Put this information to work for you and you'll soon begin experiencing fantastic results.

Celebrate Your Learning!

! *Why is it important to know that people learn in different ways?*

Knowing about different learning styles leads to clearer communication and understanding, and greater learning ability.

! *How can you categorize people when each person is an individual?*

Learning styles models are helpful generalizations and are to be used as guidelines.

! *In taking learning styles tests, what influences your choices?*

Your personality, experiences, education, and the way your brain functions, as well as your current circumstances.

! *Do different models measure the same thing?*

Models vary. Psycho-Geometrics is a global model that gives you information on how you learn, communicate, and handle situations. The Gregorc Model tells you how you think and process information. The Personal Thinking Pattern measures your preferred sequence (i.e., VAK) of taking in information, storing it, recalling it, and expressing it. However, the models have overlapping characteristics.

7

Embracing Change to Make Things Work

 What 3 things are successful people able to recognize?

 How do you teach yourself to be flexible?

 How do you begin to explore new ways to reach success?

 What keeps people from being flexible?

All is flux, nothing stays still . . . .
Nothing endures but change.
— Heraclitus (540-480 B.C.)

A s you can see from the 2,500-year-old quote above, there's nothing new about the idea that change is constant. For centuries, wise men and women have known they cannot prevent change, only adapt to it. And those who adapt most successfully, live most successfully.

In other words, successful people are flexible people. They're open-minded. They realize they can't control everything in their world, are quick to spot what works well, what can be improved, how to apply new strategies to any situation, and what needs to be discontinued.

Are you flexible? Or do you find you're reluctant to change something because you feel a need to protect your sense of dignity and identity? Resisting change makes you stagnant and reduces your chances for success.

Change What's Clearly Not Working

In business as in life, it's often difficult to recognize and admit when something isn't working. As a result, we find ourselves trying the same things over and over, even when the methods or procedures we're using obviously aren't producing the results we want.

If this sounds like you and your company, you're probably falling victim to ingrained beliefs:

- Someone told you something had to be done a certain way;
- You believe there's only one right answer;
- You don't want to admit to being wrong; or
- You figure you've done it this way for years, so why change now?

When you've invested large amounts of time and money—not to mention pride—in some project or plan, it's easy to convince yourself that it simply has to work. But if it doesn't, the sooner you can learn to be flexible and explore other strategies, the better your chances for success.

The first step to discovering new solutions is to simply admit that something isn't working. It sounds easy to do, but when you've told everyone your plans, you're likely to feel you've put your credibility and self-esteem on the line. To admit your plan needs a major overhaul can be a terrible blow to the ego. But once you admit you've got a problem, you can take the next step and start working on solutions.

One way to increase your flexibility is by detaching your ego from your actions. In other words, you must separate who you are from what you do. At Hawthorne/Stone, one of our business principles was "get off what clearly is not working." When something didn't work, we dropped it or modified it and moved on. No excuses, justifications, or long discussions, and no hard feelings. It was okay for something to not work. It meant we'd discovered one way not to do it. When that happened, we just went on to look for other new ideas to try. We realized that except for our beliefs and principles, nothing was cast in stone.

Sometimes it's hard to differentiate between when things aren't working and when you're just experiencing a temporary setback. Your gut feeling often provides the first clue your strategy needs changing. If you tune in to that feeling, then stop and measure your results, you'll have some hard data to direct you.

In my business, we gauge our success by the number of program participants we enroll. For several years, our enrollments rose steadily. Eventually, however, they stabilized. For a few more years we continued with the same marketing plan, hoping each time that the numbers would increase. Ultimately, we determined that our doldrums were partly due to the country's economic recession. But we also realized that if we wanted to put enrollments back on an upward path, we would have to make some changes. After all, if we kept doing things the same way, could we realistically expect different results?

We kept our most effective marketing strategies and added new methods as well. Making necessary changes, we rode out the recession, and despite a boost in tuition, enrollments remained steady and revenues increased.

What Might Work Better

Flexibility is also helpful when it comes to fine-tuning projects and operations that are working, but could be even more effective. The danger lies in letting complacency set in. We should continually examine our systems, products, and organization in a quest to do everything better. Take a look at some of the processes and equipment your company uses. Perhaps your current computer system works fine—but could a new, faster system help serve your customers better by saving time and keeping better track of orders?

In business, competition is increasing at a furious rate. Tomorrow you'll have more competition than today, and your rival will most likely be a company frighteningly similar to yours. These businesses will catch on to your successful ideas. The U.S. Small Business Administration reports new-business incorporations now exceed 700,000 per year, and are growing. The SBA expects that growth to continue at an accelerating rate, which is even more reason to keep flexible and stay ahead of the times.

Suspend Your Assumptions

Sometimes we block our own success by being inflexible and assuming we're right. We assume our way is the only way, so there must be something else out there blocking our success. We're sure that if we just keep trying, eventually we'll succeed. But, as Leo Tolstoy said, "Conceit is incompatible with understanding."

Most of us are also guilty of making assumptions about new ideas and judging their value before we try them. Usually, we see a situation through a particular filter that fits our belief and understanding, and assumes we're right. Getting beyond this filter means letting go of being right.

You can learn to be flexible; you can teach yourself to suspend your assumptions and listen without judgment. But before you can do this, you must get past your resistance, your natural tendency to balk at change. First, just let yourself be open to new ideas that might not fit your present picture of things. In looking at a situation, pretend you've never seen it before. Sometimes it helps to call on someone outside your business to give you an objective opinion. Ask this person to describe the situation in his own words, then notice how different the information sounds. You may discover solutions you previously overlooked, simply because you're no longer filtering the information through your own belief system.

I'm not talking about necessarily hiring a consultant. Not all situations merit the time and expense involved with calling in a professional. For example, my husband and I have a friend who has some marketing expertise. Sometimes when a marketing problem comes up, we'll just call our friend and tell him about it. He'll ask questions, raise issues, make suggestions, and maybe give a little advice. He's not acting as a full-blown consultant; more like a sounding board, an objective pair of ears. On many occasions, he's helped us to see a problem in ways we hadn't considered, or gave us a simple tip that enabled us to solve the problem. A valuable service, and it rarely costs us more than the price of a nice dinner. What makes it a true win/win situation is our friend really enjoys helping us out and contributing value to a business he believes in.

If you'd rather not call on another person, try to think of a person whose opinion you respect. Then imagine you are that person. What would he or she say about the situation? Better yet, imagine you have a board of directors that you can call upon for advice. Appoint to your board whomever you like: Lee Iacocca, Ted Turner, Albert Einstein—the best minds you can think of. Present your problem to them. What would they say? How would they solve it?

Putting Flexibility to Work

Once we admit something isn't working or could work better, we can begin to explore new ways to reach success. Flexibility means trying different approaches until we find what works best. As we try various alternatives to a procedure or operation, we begin to accumulate data. We see that certain things produce a desired result, while others don't. We discover some aspects of the current system are effective and some are worthless. The very act of trying different things tells us what will make our efforts successful.

It's important to remember we all have a choice, all the time. We can stop and think before acting, review what our choices are, and then decide on the best action. When we feel frustrated with a situation and don't know why, it just might be time for more flexibility. Sometimes, the key, which isn't always so easy, is to let go of the emotional feel-

Flexibility means trying different approaches until you find what works best.

Imagine you have a board of directors of famous people you can call upon for advice. What advice would they give you?

ings of not being successful in a particular way and accept being successful in a different way.

Taking a Risk

What keeps most people from being more flexible? For one thing, fear of the unknown. Change can be risky. There's always a chance a new idea won't work. Sometimes we feel safer using the same old methods, even when they don't get the results we want. We become anxious about what could happen with a new method. It might be better, but it could be worse—and then what?

There are still plenty of people who avoid computers, fax machines, voice mail, and the other technology most of us now take for granted—because they're afraid of trying something new. Of course, if we don't try something new, we never move forward. And if our current strategies are failing, it's clearly time to risk trying something new.

When evaluating a new strategy, discover what's at risk and decide whether you're willing to live with the worst possible outcome. How long will you keep trying before you consider other strategies? It's good to determine what that length of time is before you start. Otherwise, you'll tend to want to continue a little longer, and then a little longer until you've let it go much longer than appropriate. Ask yourself, "What are some false assumptions I've made in the past that could affect my success?" Take time to consider these assumptions before you jump into anything.

But taking risks doesn't mean putting your entire business in danger. You can define and limit your risk before you jump in. Producing our first academic summer camp was risky, since we had no way of knowing for sure how many people would be interested. Plus, the liability was high because we were working with minors. However, we started with only one program, capped the number of enrollments, and tested the waters ahead of time with market surveys and research. These measures defined and limited the amount of risk, and while we had setbacks, none of them was large enough to knock us out of business. So ultimately, we prospered.

I think of flexibility as being prepared for change and having the willingness to do things differently. When things are going well, I don't advocate change just for the sake of change. But we must be aware of the possibility of a shift in our field and be prepared to take action. Our SuperCamp programs have always been held in the summer when students are out of school, but with more school systems adopting year-round calendars, we've had to stay flexible and follow the trends. We can't think of ourselves as just a summer program. We need to think of ourselves as motivators and teachers of learning skills so that we aren't stuck in a paradigm of producing summer programs. We must be ready for change and to take another path.

American railroads nearly died out when the owners failed to understand just what business they were in. They could only see trains, trains, trains. But in reality, however, their business wasn't trains, it was the transportation of people and freight. While they weren't looking, large trucks and airplanes came along and took a huge chunk of the transportation market, and the railroads were left having to scramble to catch up. When was the last time you traveled a long distance on a train, or shipped a package by rail? Do you think you ever will again?

Beware of Complacency

To truly succeed, you must take a hard look at your business policies, processes, products—anything taken for granted—and ask yourself if there's a way to make these better. Suspend your assumptions, allow yourself to see things with new eyes, and you'll discover new approaches.

Being more flexible in your business as well as in your personal life can open up new possibilities and increase your successes. Take time to examine the areas in your life where frustration or complacency have set in; these feelings provide clues that something needs to change. Then, apply flexibility and find innovative solutions. Flexibility can be the most important key to your success.

Celebrate Your Learning!

! *What three things are successful people able to recognize?*

    1. What is working well.
    2. What could work better.
    3. What should be discontinued.

! *How do you teach yourself to be flexible?*

Be open:

- Get past your resistance.
- Suspend your assumptions.
- Listen without judgment.
- Pretend you've never seen the situation before.

! *How do you begin to explore new ways to reach success?*

Accumulate data. Try different approaches until you find what works best.

! *What keeps people from being flexible?*

Fear of the unknown. There's always a risk a new idea won't work. The risk of not changing with the times is actually riskier.

8

Secrets of High-Tech Note-Taking

 What is the main purpose of note-taking—and what other purposes can it serve?

 What is Mind Mapping and how does it work?

 What are Mindscapes?

 What is Notes:TM and how is it better than traditional note-taking?

You probably already know how to take notes . . . those hurried, incomprehensible scribbles that end up being of little or no use to you or anyone else. But what if you knew how to take notes that really meant something? Imagine taking notes that capture entire concepts, organize information, make connections between ideas, are easy to remember, and fun to take: that's the kind of note-taking this chapter focuses on. Forget the traditional outline format you learned in school. You're about to master Mind Mapping® and Notes:TM—easy, effective note-taking systems that can record volumes of information on a single page.

Who Takes Notes?

Whether you realize it or not, you probably take some kind of notes every day. It could be in the form of recording what was discussed at a meeting, jotting down the key ideas of a training seminar, or just making out your to-do list. The main purpose of note-taking is to help you understand and remember valuable information. Most of us remember things better when we write them down. A good note-taking method can help you keep track of the latest breakthroughs in your field and can also help you stay on top of the myriad projects, activities, and meetings you're involved in every day.

We've all taken notes at seminars, workshops, and meetings to record events and ideas. But besides recording information, you can also use note-taking to generate fresh ideas and organize your thoughts. You can use notes as a starting point for writing articles, reports, speeches, even your own books. They may also spark your creativity and ease mental blocks.

Mind Mapping®

You may already have been exposed to this note-taking method, which is catching on fast around the world. Developed by Tony Buzan in the early '60s, this method works well because it imitates the way your brain works. Mind Mapping engages both the left and right hemispheres of the brain. Pictures, symbols, colors, and random ordering, primarily right-hemisphere activities, are incorporated into this system, as is the left-hemisphere processing of words, logic, and sequences.

Research shows there are five key elements to making facts memorable. We learn best when information:

1. is emphasized,

2. is associated with prior learning,

3. engages our five senses,

4. has personal importance, or

5. comes at the beginning or end of the learning period.

Mind Mapping makes use of all these elements, resulting in some powerful, highly memorable note-taking!

Getting Started

First, take all your old ideas about note-taking, such as linear format, Roman numerals, single-coloring, and so on—and throw them away. You won't need any of that. Now, take a look at the Mind Map model on page 157. Notice how it starts with a central idea and branches out to include subtopics and details. The lines of the main topics are thicker to emphasize their importance. Keep in mind that these main branches are usually different colors, although this book is printed in black and white. Also notice the use of symbols and pictures to communicate thoughts. When you get the hang of Mind Mapping, you'll probably develop your own pictorial shorthand, conveying reams of information in minimal space.

One of the best things about Mind Maps is that you can keep adding thoughts as they come to mind. Linear notes, such as lists, limit our thinking. They make it difficult for us to make associations, the very process we use to generate new ideas. With Mind Maps, when we have more ideas we just add more branches, so our original Mind Map can spawn a dozen other Mind Maps. We can also make associations between two different topics by drawing an arrow between the two branches.

Practice making a few Mind Maps of your own. You can Mind Map any topic: plans for your next vacation, the last book you read, your company's departments and their responsibilities, or anything else that comes to mind. The key right now is practice.

Follow These Simple Steps

To begin, you'll need colored pens or pencils and a piece of paper. Turning your paper in a horizontal position makes it easier to create your Mind Map; it gives you more room to draw horizontal branches, which makes them easier to read.

1. *Put Your Main Topic in the Center of the Page*
   It can be a written word, a drawing, or both. Using a drawing may make the Mind Map more powerful and increase your ability to remember it, especially if you're the type who thinks better in pictures than in words (you know who you are).

2. *Draw a Thick Branch Extending Out from the Main Idea for Each of Your Subtopics or Key Points*
   Make each branch a different color, or rotate colors

I started this book by creating a Mind Map® of each chapter so I could see how all of the information fit together.

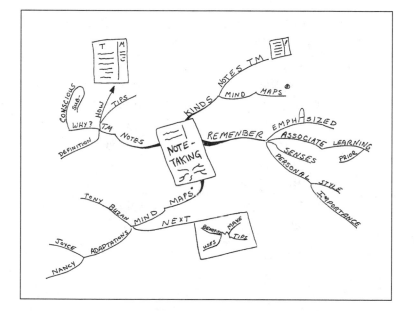

Here's my Mind Map for this chapter.

to keep it varied. Avoid making two side-by-side branches the same color; different colors help make it easier to distinguish between subtopics. Write the key word or image on top of each branch. Try to stick to one word as it provides more freedom of thought.

3. *Attach New Branches to Your Subtopics as You Come Up with Thoughts on These Areas*
    Using pictures and symbols makes your Mind Map more memorable. Place them on the line as well.

4. *When You Feel You've Completed a Branch, You May Want to Separate It from the Other Branches for Clarity.*
    You can do this by drawing an outline or wavy line around the branch, or shading the area a different color. You may discover that one of your smaller points is really a main topic that you'd like to explore further by making it a separate Mind Map. That is the nature of Mind Maps. They allow for leaps in thought and associations, and they encourage creativity.

Mind Maps are a great way to overcome mental blocks; those frustrating moments when you seem to run out of ideas. Because the brain searches for completion, you can defeat mental blocks simply by adding empty branches to your Mind Map. Your brain will naturally search for associations to fill in the blanks.

This trick is especially helpful when you're faced with a writing assignment and don't know where to begin. Make a Mind Map of your letter or article, putting your topic in the center. Ask yourself what the main points are, and make these your branches. Draw smaller branches from

To Mind Map, focus
on a central idea and
"branch" outward.

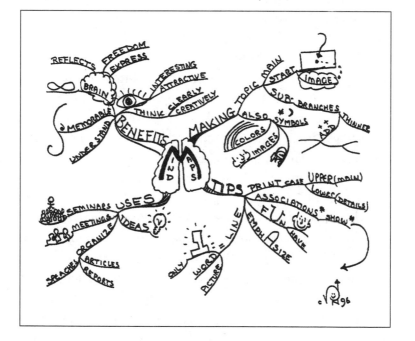

– by Vanda North

these main points, and let your mind fill in the blanks. You'll quickly have all your thoughts down on paper and will be able to then put them in order. This method is used successfully by many professional writers to get past "writer's block" and is useful for anyone in business.

Putting Mind Maps to Work

Once you and your co-workers are comfortable using Mind Maps, you'll want to start using them whenever you can. I suggest you start using Mind Maps at brainstorming sessions. It's a great way to record everyone's thoughts, get the creative juices flowing, and generate lots of fresh ideas.

At my company, we have a meeting every fall to review our summer programs. Prior to the meeting, we ask staff members to record their thoughts on individual Mind Maps. Then, we combine all the Mind Maps into one. This way, everyone's input is posted where we can all review it, and the meeting runs more efficiently.

Business consultant Joyce Wycoff has written an entire book on the business applications of Mind Maps. In *Mindmapping, Your Personal Guide to Exploring Creativity and Problem-Solving,* (Berkley Books, New York, 1991), she describes how five minutes of Mind Mapping can move you toward better project management, a method used by many businesses these days. She notes, "The increased focus on projects (versus repetitive processes) is one of the biggest changes in work life today. Everyone has become a project manager." If you feel reluctant to start a project, drawing a Mind Map can help get you going.

Starting out with a Mind Map gives you direction, and it can make overwhelming projects more manageable. A Mind Map forces you to break a project down into smaller chunks, or subprojects, thereby making it easier to master.

Six Tips for Mind Mapping:

1 **Print neatly.** Emphasize words through under-lining, highlighting, and thick lines.

2 **Show associations by drawing an arrow between branches.**

3 **Personalize your Mind Map by relating infor-mation to your own experiences.** I find there's something personal about the process of making Mind Maps. Creating my own Mind Map forces me to come up with my own symbols and connec-tions, cementing the information in my memory.

4 **Develop your own shorthand of symbols, pictures, and abbreviations.**

5 **Unleash your natural artistic ability.** Add lots of pictures to your Mind Map. Your drawings will improve with practice.

6 **When you've completed your Mind Map, you may want to put the information in either chronological order or in order of importance.** To do this, simply number each branch. On my own Mind Maps, I always start my first branch in the upper right, the one o'clock position, and continue clockwise. This way, my information is already in order, and when I review my Mind Maps I always know where to start.

You can then calculate your action steps and divide the subprojects among co-workers.

Making a project management Mind Map is really quite simple. Use the usual Mind Map format, putting your main topic in the center with subtopics branching out. Then, in the upper left corner, write WWWWWH$. This stands for Who, What, When, Where, Why, How and Money. Wycoff suggests referring to this list while making your Mind Map. Ask yourself: Who needs to be involved in the project, What resources are needed, When does it need to be completed, What costs are involved, and other related questions.

Asking these questions will help you think through the project thoroughly. It will also spur you to overcome any mental blocks. Once you've completed your Mind Map, it's easy to move forward with your project.

Mindscapes

Mindscapes are an outgrowth of Mind Mapping. Developed by Nancy Margulies, corporate consultant and author, this method goes beyond the rules of Mind Mapping, allowing further individuality. Once you've mastered Mind Mapping, you may want to experiment with this unique method.

Steps

1. The first rule of Mindscapes is, it's okay to break the rules. Breaking rules encourages creativity.

2. Start anywhere on the page. A Mindscape doesn't necessarily need a central image; it's a more free-flowing form of visual mapping, so do whatever works.

Mindscaping is a note-taking method drawing on your individuality.

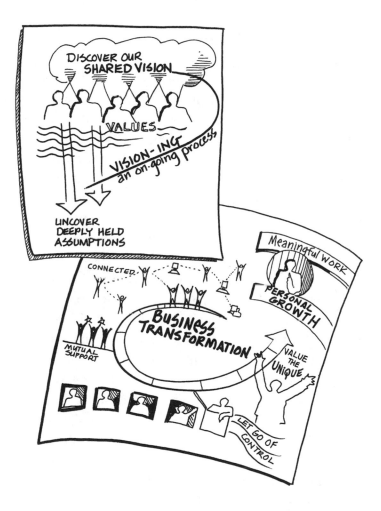

Nancy Margulies developed this unique method of recording information in a highly visual format.

3. Mindscape images may incorporate words, phrases, quotations, even photos or pictures from magazines.

4. Vary your Mindscapes as much as possible. Experiment with different forms. Develop your own style.

Notes:TM

Notes:TM is a variation of Cornell Notes, and was developed by Learning Forum's Training Director, Mark Reardon. The TM stands for 'T'aking and 'M'aking. Note-Taking is writing down the information you want to remember. Note-Making is writing down your own thoughts and impressions about that information. Putting the two together helps you focus on the information at hand and makes it more meaningful for you. (As we mentioned, one of the keys to remembering something is giving it personal importance.)

Here's a common situation where Notes:TM could come to the rescue. Picture a typical company meeting. It's three o'clock in the afternoon, and you're feeling a little drowsy. The speakers drone on and on about financial statements. What they have to say is important, but your mind keeps drifting. You think about what you ate for lunch, what you'll do after work, even your own projects, anything but the meeting. Suddenly, you notice the room is quiet. The CEO turns to you and says, "What's your opinion on this situation?" Desperately, you search your notes for a clue of what was said, but all you find is a blank page.

Why does our mind drift despite our best efforts to pay attention? Because the average person's normal speaking rate doesn't keep up with our brain's ability to process information. The normal speaking rate is approximately

Mindscaping continues to be recognized for its value.

Nancy Margulies is a visual mapper with clout. As a consultant, she has Mindscaped meetings for hundreds of companies, including Xerox, Boeing, and Hewlett-Packard. She also teaches Mindscaping and mapping at seminars and conferences.

I once scheduled Nancy to Mindscape at the annual Accelerative Learning and Teaching conference. As president of the International Alliance for Learning, I knew Nancy would add much to the conference. Unfortunately, someone else also wanted her talents. Two weeks before the conference, I received a call from Nancy. Apologetically, she told me she wouldn't be able to make it. She'd received an invitation to map a meeting for someone she couldn't turn down: President Clinton.

Nancy Mindscaped a cabinet retreat meeting that included the President, Vice-President, and members of the Cabinet. Nancy says she was called in because "They wanted to be able to convey the essence of the discussion to their own staffs and experience sharing information in both an auditory and visual way. They understood that it is necessary to reach people on many levels."

I was sorry she missed my conference, but really couldn't blame her. For most of us, an invitation to present our work to the President is a once in a lifetime experience.

200 to 300 words per minute. Our brains are able to process auditory information at 600 to 800 words per minute. Because of the lag-time created and our minds' ability to make associations, we're able to think about all sorts of things while listening to someone speak. Notes:TM can help you turn your mind's wanderings to your advantage.

By writing down both the speaker's information and your own thoughts and impressions about what's being said, you're focusing both your conscious and subconscious mind. When you're focusing on the speaker's words and writing down factual data, you're using your conscious mind. The subconscious is where you make associations, form impressions, reactions, or new applications to the information. Writing down your subconscious thoughts helps you keep focused on the task at hand.

Recent studies have shown the effectiveness of this technique. Win Wenger, a learning and creativity consultant, conducted experiments on a note-taking method he calls Freenoting™. Students were told to write rapidly in the context of the topic, even if they were sure they knew nothing about it! As they wrote, they were to consciously ignore the lecture being presented. The study showed that these students still wrote down clear notes on the lecture topic. In fact, they usually put down more and better information than the lecturer had presented! According to Wenger, "The exercise locks in and makes richly memorable the essential contents of the lecture. By consciously ignoring the lecturer's words, the Freenoter was sending the contents of what the lecturer was saying directly to the subconscious." Ignoring the lecture frees the mind, allowing for associations and connections that might be missed if the student were consciously paying attention. Associations made in the subconscious mind made the

Notes:TM helps you focus both your conscious and subconscious mind.

Notes:TM

T is for 'T'aking
Writing down the information you
want to remember

M is for 'M'aking
Writing down your own thoughts
and impressions

lecture much more memorable than if the students had simply listened on a conscious level.

Notes:TM—How to Do It

On a sheet of paper, draw a vertical line dividing the sheet so that three-quarters of the page is to the left of the line. Now, use the larger left side for Note-Taking—copying down what's being said. The right-hand side is where you jot down your own impressions about the information—Note-Making.

Let's say you're in a meeting and someone is proposing a new marketing strategy. As you record the target market, projected returns, and so forth down the left side of your page, your right-hand notes might be something like "Will that really work? . . . How do I fit into this? . . . Call John to check on those numbers . . . Maybe this will jibe with our other products . . . That's a crazy idea!"

Use two different colored pens and switch colors whenever the speaker changes topics. This will make it easier to remember your notes and to review them later on.

At the end of the meeting, quickly go over your notes. Use a highlighter to mark important points. Develop a system of symbols and use these for identifying key information. You might use an exclamation mark for important points, a star for subtopics, and a dollar sign for financials. Again, adding symbols and pictures to your notes will make them easier to remember and it will also help you locate important information when you review your notes.

Try a few practice exercises so you get the hang of using Notes:TM. For instance, take notes on a book you're reading, recording key points and your own impressions. Or take notes while listening to a taped lecture, a radio show, or while watching the news. Experiment with

Adding symbols and pictures to your notes will make them easier to remember.

Note-Taking	Note-Making
🔑 KEY POINTS: text, text, text, text, text, text, text, text, text, text, text, text, text, text, text, text, text,	Impressions . . . etc, etc, etc, etc, etc, etc, etc, etc
INFORMATION: text, text, text text, text, text, text, text, text, text, text, text, text, text, text, text, text, text, text, text,	Thoughts . . . etc, etc, etc, etc, etc, etc, etc. ♥
FACT: text, text, text, text, text, text, text, text, text, text, text, text, text, text, $ text, text, text, text, text, text, text.	Will this really work? etc, etc, etc, etc, etc, etc, etc, etc
FACT: text, text, text, text, text, text, text, text, text, ! text, text, text, text, text, text, text, text, text, text.	

various colors and symbols. Soon you'll be up to speed and ready for your important business meeting.

Notes:TM Tips

1. *Record Your Feelings/Emotions about Information* (boring, sad, exciting, etc.). Creating an emotional relationship to the information makes it easier to recall.

2. *Personalize Your Notes with Symbols and Pictures* Develop your own system of symbols.

3. *Review the Highlighted Portions of Your Notes Periodically to Cement Them in Your Memory*

4. *Follow Up on Any Ideas Recorded on Either Side of Your Page* Your subconscious ramblings just may be the beginning of something great!

Practice, Practice, Practice

Mind Mapping, Mindscaping, and Notes:TM may feel awkward to you at first. You may worry that you're missing valuable information by just drawing a picture or jotting down your feelings. When I first started Mind Mapping, I wasn't sure it was going to work. But I committed to trying it for one week, and I practiced every chance I got. I Mind Mapped books, articles, speeches, anything I could. During that process, the method became easy and natural. I recommend you also commit yourself to a week of trying Mind Mapping, Mindscaping, or Notes:TM. The more you practice these skills, the easier and more natural they'll become.

Celebrate Your Learning!

! *What is the main purpose of note-taking and what other purposes can it serve?*

Its main purpose is to help you understand and remember valuable information. But it can also help you generate fresh ideas, organize your thoughts, spark your creativity, and help you overcome mental blocks.

! *What is Mind Mapping and how does it work?*

It is a note-taking method that works by imitating the way the brain works in order to make your notes more memorable, useful, and valuable.

! *What are Mindscapes?*

These are a more free-flowing form of visual mapping, allowing for further individuality.

! *What is Notes:TM and how is it better than traditional note-taking?*

Notes:TM stands for Note-Taking and Note-Making. It's better because it distinguishes between noting the information you receive (note-taking) and your reactions to it (note-making).

9

The Value of Ownership

 What is "Pride of Ownership" and and how does it benefit you in your work?

 What does it mean to play "Above the Line" or "Below the Line"?

 What are ways to take responsibility for your communications?

 How do you take ownership of your learning?

T he well-known term "Pride of Ownership" refers to the way people tend to take special care of things that belong to them. Have you ever noticed how teenagers treat their cars? They wash and polish their "wheels" to a showroom shine, even if the car is a 15-year-old clunker with 200,000 miles on it. They're proud because they own the car.

That same pride of ownership can influence each of us in everything we do. At work, if we feel a sense of ownership in our work and our company, we're more likely to do the best job we can.

In the 8 Keys, we define ownership as taking responsibility for our actions. Sounds simple enough. Unless of course we believe that someone or something outside of us is in control of our lives. We often resort to this thinking when things go wrong in our lives. It's easier to blame some outside culprit than it is to admit we made a mistake.

Games are a good example of this. Have you ever found yourself losing at a game or sport and making excuses for the loss? Some of the more popular excuses are: "This is the first time I've played," or "That's not the way I play this game." Or how about "The sun was in my eyes," or "I never liked this game anyway." It's funny to hear the excuses we come up with over something as trivial as winning—or losing—a silly game.

This behavior isn't so humorous when it carries over into our work and personal lives, however. In fact, it can be seriously damaging. Blaming co-workers, spouses, or society in general for our problems rarely leads to a solution, and can gravely hurt relationships. In these cases, we may think we're relieving ourselves of responsibility for our actions, but in reality, nobody wins.

Ownership:
Taking responsibility
for your actions.

When you feel a sense

of ownership,

you take responsibility,

give your best effort,

and take pride

in the results.

Playing the Ownership Game

There are two ways to play the game of ownership:

1. Playing Above the Line and

2. Playing Below the Line.

Look at the diagram on the page to the right. Above the Line are responsibility, choices, and freedom. Playing Above the Line means being accountable for your actions and willing to make corrections when necessary. It means looking at your options, choosing solutions, and finding ways to become more effective. Above the Line thinking leads to greater freedom. You're not just sitting back and accepting failure; you're using your experiences to move you toward success. Rather than being controlled by circumstances, you determine your own actions.

If you miss the deadline on a report and you're playing Above the Line, you might say to your boss, or whoever needs the report: "I haven't completed the report, and I apologize. I'll have it done tomorrow. Is there anything I can do now that would help? I could call others and let them know when to expect the report. I could get you the sections I've already completed. And I'll do my best to have future reports done on time."

Below the Line are justification, laying blame, denial, and giving up. All seem handy alternatives to responsibility.

Justifying is coming up with a reason why you didn't perform as expected: "I didn't have the right equipment," or "Other projects came up and I ran out of time." Below the Line thinking tries to provide reasons for failure, believing that the reason or excuse will make everything okay.

Laying blame is the easiest and perhaps the most damaging form of Below the Line thinking. When you say,

Playing "Above the Line" —

Choices

Freedom

Accountability

Solutions

Responsibility

Willingness

Justification

Laying blame

Denial

Giving up

Reasons

— playing "Below the Line"

"John didn't get me his data so I couldn't complete the report," you may think it's a viable excuse, but it doesn't solve the problem. And consider what happens when your story gets back to John. It's sure to cause bad feelings, and may even set you up for John to blame you when something goes amiss later.

Denying your responsibility doesn't make the problem go away. Statements like, "What report? I didn't know I was supposed to work on that report. I never agreed to that," are obviously ineffective. They can cause others lots of frustration, and make you seem unreliable or even dishonest.

Giving up on the whole situation is another way of playing Below the Line. When you're so sure you'll fail that you don't even bother to try, you sabotage your chances for success before you've even begun. That kind of thinking gives you an excuse for your failure. You deceive and diminish yourself when you say, "I knew I couldn't do it, so I didn't try very hard. It's not important, anyway."

When you play Above the Line, you take responsibility for your life. You begin to make things happen. You have greater control because you stop blaming things outside yourself for your current situation. You can take ownership of your career, relationships, financial status, education, or other areas of your life. You can create a huge shift in your life simply by taking ownership of your attitude.

Taking ownership also means not blaming others for what happens to you. Blaming your parents, financial status, or lack of education only leads to dead ends. Think of responsibility as "respond-ability." The ability to respond to what happens to you, rather than just accept it. It takes action to make things happen.

Ownership Through Communication

We can take ownership of our lives every day, in many different ways. For example, we can demonstrate that we're taking ownership simply by the way we communicate. Recently, I was 20 minutes late for an important meeting on the other side of town. When I arrived, I could clearly see the person waiting for me was upset. I started to put the blame on the traffic. Instead, I said, "I'm late because I got stuck in traffic. I knew there might be heavy traffic this time of day, and I should have left earlier. I'm sorry and I realize I cost you time waiting for me. Would you like me to stay later than we'd planned? Next time I'll leave earlier." Instantly, I saw the anger melt away from my associate's face. My taking ownership defused his anger. It made him realize I was sincere in my apology.

You may have recognized that I used the four-part apology to express myself clearly. We also used it in our first example of playing Above the Line. Anytime you need to take ownership of a situation that deserves an apology, you can use the Four-Part Apology described in Chapter 3. (1. Acknowledge, 2. Apologize, 3. Make It Right, 4. Recommit.) You acknowledge you're responsible for your behavior and its consequences or costs to others. You say you're sorry. Then you look for a way to make it right, and commit to appropriate behavior in the future. Use this method whenever you find yourself making excuses.

The Tahoe Group, a partnership of learning consultants, developed a method for people to use to take ownership of their communication and agreements with others. They call it The Awareness Game™. To go through the entire process here would require a book in itself, and I could hardly do it justice. However, you can begin to apply the four basic rules of that game in your life.

Those rules are:

1. Be Clear   Clarify your objectives.
Set attainable goals.

2. Be Fair   Satisfy concerns and be equitable to all involved.

3. Be Truthful   Only make agreements that you can and will keep. You may be willing to do some things but not able—or able but not willing.

4. Be Responsible Follow through and do your part. Evaluate the results.

A friend of mine recently used this method when a business deal turned sour. Sarah was having cash flow problems, so she decided to refinance her condominium with the help of her friend, George. They decided George would refinance using his financial statement and would make all payments. In return, Sarah would repay George an amount equal to these payments within five years. At the end of five years, they would sell the condo and split the profits.

Two years into the deal, George wanted out. Payments on his adjustable-rate loan were rising steadily, and he felt he could no longer afford it. He told Sarah "I can't keep making these payments. You're on your own."

Sarah was disappointed that George broke his agreement, but wanted to work toward a fair solution. She told George, "How would you feel if you were no longer responsible for payments and got back everything you paid so far? In order to do that, I'll have to sell the condo now. I'll give you what you paid plus $5,000." (Be Clear)

Sarah didn't like having to move three years earlier than planned, and she needed extra money to start over. But she

The Awareness Game has four basic rules: Be clear, be fair, be truthful, and be responsible.

The Awareness Game™
The Tahoe Group
Jane Wanger, Co-founder

also wanted to make sure they had a clear agreement that was satisfactory to both of them. (Be Fair) To do this, they both had to tell the truth about what they would be willing and able to do.

In the end, they both agreed it would be best to sell the condo immediately. Sarah asked George to continue making the payments until it was sold, and he agreed. (Be Truthful) They decided George would receive 30% of the profits and Sarah would receive 70%. This way, George would recover the money he'd invested and make a profit, and Sarah would be compensated for the early move. In evaluating the situation, Sarah acknowledged she was stressed financially, and also realized she didn't get a written contract. (Be Responsible) Applying the four rules, Sarah took ownership for working out a new agreement that was fair to both parties.

Ownership of Projects

I've found people are more likely to take ownership of something when they strongly believe in it, or when the stakes are high. A project manager who is committed and excited about a project and knows the success or failure will largely be attributed to him, is likely to do whatever it takes to bring his project to fruition. He'll feel responsible for it every step of the way. He'll make sure that work delegated to others is completed and that deadlines are met. He'll likely be willing to stay late or work weekends to get it done. Others on the team may not share his level of commitment because they're not ultimately responsible. However, you get the best results when everyone takes ownership of and finds value in what they do.

Own Your Education

In the business world, you're constantly faced with the

challenge of learning something new, as are people in many other careers. If you choose to own that task— respond to it instead of reacting to it—you'll be much more likely to succeed. And, the more knowledge and skills you have, the more numerous your career options will be.

When you don't own the learning process, it shows up in physical responses. Walk into any seminar and you'll see participants slumped in their chairs, heads hanging down while they doodle, yawn, or talk to their neighbors. Some people have such ingrained negative ideas about learning that this physical response has actually become a reflex for them.

To demonstrate how your physiology affects your attitude, try this experiment: Hunch your shoulders forward, slump down in your chair, and look at the floor. Now try to feel excited and inspired to take on the world!

It can't be done.

Now try this: Roll your shoulders back, sit up straight, and keep your chin up. While maintaining this position, try to feel depressed.

It can't be done.

You can influence your attitude about learning just by adjusting your physiology. Make your outlook learning-friendly. Change your posture. Make the effort to sit and stand straight, look up, and take a deep breath. This makes it easier to maintain a positive outlook.

At SuperCamp, we teach students to SLANT. This is an acronym for Sit up, Lean forward, Ask questions, Nod your head, and Talk to your teacher. (It also helps to sit in the front row.) Sitting up and leaning forward makes it easy to focus your attention and actually raises your interest level. Asking questions, nodding, and talking to the teacher after class get you actively involved in the learning process.

After a while, adjusting your physiology (and your attitude) becomes a reflex. There are two types of reflexes:

1. Involuntary, such as breathing, blinking, or the release of adrenaline in response to fear; and

2. Learned, such as flinching from a raised hand, or salivating at the sound of the dinner bell.

A learned reflex is a conditioned response. Remember Pavlov's dogs? Every time Pavlov fed his dogs, he rang a bell. Eventually, the dogs associated the sound of the bell with food. They would salivate every time the bell rang, even when no food was present.

You may not be able to control everything that happens in your life, but you can control your reactions. You can condition yourself to adopt more positive responses.

Ownership is empowering. It means accepting the responsibility for making choices that will ultimately lead to greater freedom. Taking ownership of a problem leads to solutions.

How will you play the game of ownership—Above the Line or Below the Line? You face this decision in dozens of situations every day. Whatever the circumstances, whatever the situation, taking responsibility and being accountable for your actions is the best strategy for success.

Celebrate Your Learning!

! *What is "Pride of Ownership" and how does it benefit you in your work?*

Pride of Ownership is the tendency to take special care of things that belong to you. You can have this feeling about anything you value, not just material goods. It benefits you by making you more likely to do your best.

! *What does it mean to play "Above the Line" or "Below the Line"?*

In the ownership game, playing "Above the Line" means being accountable for your actions. Playing "Below the Line" means avoiding responsibility.

! *What are ways to take responsibility for your communications?*

By taking ownership of your actions and using the Four-Part Apology. Also remember the basic rules of the Awareness Game: Be clear, be fair, be truthful, and be responsible.

! *How do you take ownership of your learning?*

First through your physical responses. Walk and sit tall. Second, through your attitude. Respond to your task with a positive attitude, rather than react to it. You can also organize your work space, listen to music, exercise, and take frequent breaks.

10

The Power to Read Your Best

 What are three key ways to increase speed and comprehension?

 Why is an alpha brain wave state beneficial for reading?

 How can you increase your peripheral vision?

 What one thing can you do that will double your reading speed?

Time. There just never seems to be enough of it. The current increase in two-career households leaves more and more of us juggling jobs, family, physical fitness, friendships, community service, and education. With so many commitments to fulfill, it's no wonder we sometimes drop the ball.

One of the balls we drop more than the others is the stack of reading material that seems to be breeding and reproducing itself in the corner. "If I only had the time to read," you say to yourself, "I could keep abreast of business trends, new policies at work, reports from the board, and other valuable information I need. But how can I create time? There are only so many hours . . . "

True, you can't create time; there are only so many hours in a day. If all you have is 20 minutes a day for informational reading, but you really need two hours, you'll just keep falling farther and farther behind. On the other hand, if you could increase your speed and comprehension so that you got two hours' worth of reading done in 20 minutes, not only would you breeze through that stack of papers, you'd also free up more time for other aspects of life you may be neglecting—time with your family, leisure, or fitness.

Perhaps there's something you've been yearning to do, but you've kept putting it off because there doesn't seem to be time. Maybe it's going back to school. You've told yourself that with a full-time job you just can't do it. But what if you could breeze through your homework assignments in a few minutes? What possibilities would that open up?

If you learn to use whole brain Quantum Reading skills explained in this chapter, you'll not only save lots of time, you'll also get your life in better balance. Plus, the large amounts of information you'll be able to absorb in a short

Mastery of Quantum Reading skills has many benefits.

What's In It For Me:

Read more in less time

::

Increase your comprehension
and recall

::

Gain opportunities

::

Get your life in balance

time will open up opportunities both at work and at home. The faster you read, the easier it is to keep all those balls in the air without dropping any.

Steve Snyder, international trainer and consultant, reads four books per night in addition to all his "To Read" materials from work. He reads at a rate of about 5,000 words per minute—10,000 when he's in a hurry. His mother taught him to read when he was two, and by the time he entered first grade, he was reading at a high school level. He began speed-reading when he was 12, using techniques he had developed himself. Soon he was teaching his friends how to cut their study time in half with speed-reading.

We all have the capacity to read as quickly as Steve. In fact, our brains want to read quickly, but we usually slow things down, thinking that if we read slowly, we'll understand the material better. In reality, this can have the opposite effect. Reading slowly can be boring, and when we slow down our minds wander and we miss information.

Have you ever read something you urgently needed to know when time was short, like information for a report or license exam? When you studied as your deadline loomed, you probably shut out all distractions and focused completely on your material. You read as if your life depended on it, or at least your career. And with that high level of focus you retained more information than usual. You were focused because you were interested in succeeding.

We all read better and retain more when our interest is high. Quantum Reading is based on the concept of recapturing a highly focused state each time we read. Fast reading requires this high level of focused concentration, because it's when our minds are engaged and active that comprehension increases.

Quantum Reading uses both sides of the brain more effectively. Brain researchers agree that we only use a very small fraction of our brain's potential. By employing both the left and right hemispheres, we can use more of that potential, increasing speed and comprehension to higher levels than we ever thought possible.

When we read, we primarily use the left hemisphere. This is the logical, analytical hemisphere, which we use for language tasks like writing and reading. The right hemisphere is holistic, rhythmic, colorful, imaginative, and creative. To effectively engage the right hemisphere while reading, we need to use a few Quantum Reading strategies. For example, try visualizing the material, listening to baroque music while you read, or making the material more meaningful by relating it to something in your own life. Getting into a relaxed, focused state also helps you use both sides of your brain.

But before we delve into the reading process, let's measure your current reading rate. When you've completed this chapter, rate yourself again and compare the two scores to see how much your reading has improved. To do this exercise, you'll need a stopwatch or an electronic wristwatch with a chronometer to time yourself. Read the following article excerpt for one minute exactly, then mark the last line you read. Start now.

The Einstein Factor

by Win Wenger, Ph.D., and Richard Poe

Today, those numinous eyes, bushy mustache, and shock of silver hair remain the quintessential image of "genius," the name a synonym for supernormal intelligence. But as a child, Albert Einstein appeared deficient.

Dyslexia caused him difficulty in speech and reading.   5

"Normal childhood development proceeded slowly," recalled his sister. "He had such difficulty with language that they feared that he would never learn to speak. . . . Every sentence he uttered, he repeated to himself, softly, moving his lips. This habit persisted into his seventh   10 year."

Later, poor language skills provoked his Greek teacher to tell the boy, "You will never amount to anything." Einstein was expelled from high school. He flunked a college entrance exam. After finally completing his bachelor's degree, he failed to attain a recommendation from   15 his professors and was forced to take a lowly job in the Swiss patent office. Until his mid-20's, he seemed destined for a life of mediocrity. Yet, when he was 26, Einstein published his Special Theory of Relativity. Sixteen years later, he won a Nobel prize.   20

What did Einstein have that we don't? That's what Dr. Thomas Harvey wanted to know. He was the pathologist on duty at Princeton Hospital when Einstein died in 1955. By sheer chance, fate had fingered Harvey to perform Einstein's autopsy. Without permission from the   25 family, Harvey took it upon himself to remove and keep Einstein's famous brain. For the next 40 years, Harvey stored the brain in jars of formaldehyde, studying it slice by slice under the microscope and dispersing small samples to other researchers on request.   30

"Nobody had ever found a difference that earmarked a brain as that of a genius," Harvey later explained to a reporter. Neither he nor his colleagues found any definitive sign that would mark Einstein's brain as extraordinary according to the ideas of brain physiology of that   35 time. But in the early 1980's, Marian Diamond, a neu-

roanatomist at the University of California at Berkeley, made some discoveries about brains in general and Einstein's in particular that could revolutionize ideas about genius and help entrepreneurs who want to become   40
more innovative.

One of Diamond's experiments was with rats. One group she placed in a super-stimulating environment with swings, ladders, treadmills, and toys. The other group was confined to bare cages. The rats in the big-   45
stimulus environment not only lived to the advanced age of 3 (the equivalent of 90 in a man), but their brains increased in size, sprouting new glial cells, which make connections between neurons (nerve cells). As long ago as 1911, Santiago Ramón y Cajal, the father of neu-   50
roanatomy had found that the number of interconnections between neurons was a far better predictor of brain power than the sheer number of neurons.

So, in rats, Diamond had created the physical footprint of higher intelligence through mental exercise. She then   55
examined sections of Einstein's brain—and found that it, too, was unusually "interconnected." It had a larger-than-normal number of glial cells in the left parietal lobe, which is a kind of neurological switching station that connects the various areas of the brain. It has long been   60
known that unlike neurons, which do not reproduce after we are born, the connective hardware of the brain—glial cells, axons, and dendrites—can increase in number throughout life, depending on how you use your brain. The more we learn, the more of these pathways are cre-   65
ated. When we learn a skill such as riding a bicycle, we create connections between brain cells that remain for decades. Mental power is, in a way, connective power.

A "Retarded" Achievement

Was Einstein's mental development affected by some 70
analogy to the swings, ladders, treadmills, and toys of
Diamond's super-rats? Did he, in some sense, *learn* his
inventive mental powers? Einstein himself seemed to
think so. He believed that you could stimulate ingenious
thought by allowing the imagination to float freely, form- 75
ing associations at will. For instance, he attributed his
Theory of Relativity not to any special gift, but to what
he called his "retarded" development.

"A normal adult never stops to think about problems of
space and time," he said. "These are things which he has 80
thought of as a child. But my intellectual development
was retarded, and I began to wonder about space and
time only when I had already grown up."

In his *Autobiographical Notes,* Einstein recalled having the first crucial insight that led to his Special Theory 85
of Relativity at age 16 while he was daydreaming.

As a boy, Einstein had a favorite uncle named Jakob
who used to teach him mathematics. "Algebra is a merry
science," said Jakob once. "We go hunting for a little animal whose name we don't know, so we call it x. When 90
we bag our game, we pounce on it and give it its right
name." Uncle Jakob's words stayed with Einstein for the
rest of his life. They encapsulated his attitude toward
mathematical and scientific problems, which to Einstein
always seemed more like puzzles or games than work. 95
Einstein could focus on his math studies with the concentration most children reserve for play.

"What would it be like," Einstein wondered, "to run
beside a light beam at the speed of light?" Normal adults
would squelch such a question or forget it. Einstein was 100
different. He played with this question for 10 years. The

more he pondered, the more questions arose. Suppose, he asked himself, that you were riding on the end of a light beam and held a mirror before your face. Would you see your reflection? 105

According to classical physics, you would not— because light leaving your face would have to travel faster than light in order to reach the mirror. But Einstein could not accept this. It didn't feel right. It seemed ludicrous that you would look into a mirror and see nothing. 110 Einstein imagined rules for a universe that would allow you to see your reflection in a mirror while riding a light beam. Only years later did he undertake proving his theory mathematically.

Einstein attributed his scientific prowess to what he 115 called a "vague play" with "signs," "images," and other elements, both "visual" and "muscular." "This comminatory play," he wrote, "seems to be the essential feature in productive thought."

My project of the last 25 years has been to develop 120 techniques and mental exercises, based in part on Einstein's methods, that work in the short term and also develop the mind's permanent powers.

Einstein is the most spectacular modern example of a man who could dream while wide awake. With few 125 exceptions, the great discoveries in science were made through such intuitive "thought experiments."

Inventor Elias Howe labored long and hard to create the first sewing machine. Nothing worked. One night, Howe had a nightmare. He was running from a band of 130 cannibals—they were so close, he could see their spear tips. Despite his terror, Howe noticed each spear point had a hole bored in its tip like the eye of a sewing needle.

When he awoke, Howe realized what his nightmare   135
was trying to say: On his sewing machine, he needed to
move the eyehole from the middle of the needle down to
the tip. That was his breakthrough, and the sewing
machine was born.

Insights from dreams have inspired rulers, artists, sci-   140
entists, and inventors since Biblical times. But day after
day, year after year, the vast majority of people squelch
their most profound insights without even knowing it.
This defensive reflex—which I call The Squelcher—
blocks us from achieving our full potential.   145

But dreams have their limitations. They are notorious-
ly hard to control. We have not yet learned how to sum-
mon them at will. And, most of the time, we forget them.

In March 1977, a group of us had heard about the revolutionary experiments Russian scientists were making   150
by tapping the subconscious for accelerated learning.
Although no one at that time had published reliable
accounts of the exact procedures, we reconstructed these
as best we could from odd corners of the scientific literature. We decided to conduct an experiment in a friend's   155
apartment in Arlington, Va.

We were completely surprised. Nearly every technique
produced striking results for almost everyone in the
group. Especially memorable was the experience of a
participant whom I shall call "Mary." Like all of us, she   160
had agreed to embark upon some new learning experience just prior to the workshop. She chose the violin.
Mary had her first lesson just one week before our experiment. Until that time, she had never touched a violin in
her life.   165

The week following our workshop, Mary had her second lesson. She worked as a secretary in a Washington

office and had only a moderate amount of time to practice. Nevertheless, after Mary had played a few minutes, her astonished instructor announced that he was going to reenroll her in his advanced class! At our second experimental workshop, just a few weeks later, Mary gave a fine concert with her violin.

Mary owed her precocious ability to the "Raikov Effect." Using deep hypnosis, Soviet psychiatrist Dr. Vladimir Raikov made people think that they had become some great genius in history. When he "reincarnated" someone as Rembrandt, the person could draw with great facility. Later, the subject remembered nothing. Many would scoff in disbelief when shown artwork they had done under hypnosis.

Raikov demonstrated that talents unleashed under hypnosis left significant effects even after the sessions. So the method was more than an experimental oddity. It was a practical tool for learning. Moreover, as we were to discover, it could be achieved without the aid of hypnosis.

Find the number of lines you read and multiply that by nine. This is your current reading speed.

If you would like to read the rest of this article, see the November 1995 issue of *Success* magazine. It was excerpted from the book, *The Einstein Factor* (Prima Publishing, Rocklin, California, 1995).

Now you're ready to master the six steps to Quantum Reading: Prepare, State, Eyes and Hands, SuperScan, Read, and Review. We'll first explain each step in detail, then put them all together in a Quantum Reading practice session.

Step One: Prepare

To read at top speeds, we first need to prepare our minds and our reading area. We prepare our minds by reviewing our reading ABCs—Attitude, Belief, and Curiosity.

Attitude

Attitude includes both your feelings about something and the conscious adjustment of your physical posture to reflect those feelings. Before you can read at top speeds, you must think and act like a Quantum Reader.

If you dislike reading or find it a chore, you must first dump all the old negative ideas you may be carrying around with you. Imagine yourself tossing away thoughts such as, "I'm a slow reader; I hate reading; I always did poorly at reading in school; I hate those boring reports I have to read; I get embarrassed when I have to read to others." Open the window, pretend you're physically picking up these thoughts one by one, then "toss" them out and watch them drift away. Be sure all your old ideas have been tossed. Then, sit up straight, tall and proud. Adjust your posture to reflect your new attitude. Open your mind to new possibilities and get ready to take on some new beliefs.

Belief

As with most Quantum Learning activities, to read faster and comprehend better you need to engage the limitless power of your mind. You must believe that you can do it; you can change the way you read; you can read four books a night if you choose to. In the words of Henry Ford, "If you believe you can, you can, and if you believe you can't, you can't. Either way, you are right."

Replace the old beliefs you just tossed out with these

Think and act like a Quantum Reader.

Begin with the ABCs:

Attitude –

Sit up and open your mind to new possibilities

Belief –

Replace old beliefs with new, positive thoughts, such as "I am a powerful reader"

Curiosity –

Ask questions. Curiosity increases your focus.

new, positive, effective thoughts: "I am a powerful reader! I read quickly and understand thoroughly." Close your eyes, relax, and repeat these words out loud. Let them sink into your subconscious mind. Imagine yourself powering through business reports quickly and effortlessly. See yourself having time to read the newspaper and trade publications, and being up to date on the latest breakthroughs in your field. How much time can you save through Quantum Reading and how will you spend it? Believe in the power and potential of using your whole brain, and you'll read faster and with greater comprehension than you could ever have imagined.

Curiosity

Use the power of curiosity to get more out of your reading. As you get ready to read, ask questions. "Why am I reading this? What do I expect to learn?" If you ask specific questions about the material, answers will pop out at you as you read. As your mind hunts for the answers, your comprehension increases. I attended a lecture given by Paul Scheele, author of *The PhotoReading Whole Mind System* (Learning Strategies Corporation, Wayzata, Minnesota, 1993). He said, "Reading is predicting. You could be wrong, and it doesn't matter. It gets you thinking about the material. Ask yourself, 'What would I say if I were going to write this book.'"

Once you've completed the ABCs, you're mentally prepared for Quantum Reading. The next step is to prepare your reading area. You'll need good lighting, a comfortable chair, a table to support your book, and colored pens and paper for taking notes. You may also want to include a highlighter, if you like highlighting in your books. I find highlighting to be a great time saver; when I review a book, I simply superscan the highlighted areas.

Preparing your reading area supports your reading success.

Step Two: State

Focused concentration is a key ingredient if you want to read at Quantum rates and understand what you read. It's part of the state of being a Quantum Reader. In earlier chapters we mentioned how people learn more quickly and easily when they're in a relaxed, focused state. To focus your mind you need to access the alpha brain wave state. The alpha state is one of four states of brain wave activity measured on an electroencephalograph (EEG). As you may know, electrical activity in the brain fluctuates from high to low. Here's a quick rundown on the four brain wave states and their corresponding activities.

Beta

You are awake, alert, and active. In beta, your brain is attending to many different stimuli at once and activity is scattered. You may be thinking of many things at the same time or jumping from one activity to another.

Alpha

A state of relaxed concentration or daydreaming. You're absorbing material and focused on just one activity, such as playing a challenging game of chess. This is the state we want to access for optimum Quantum Reading.

Theta

Brain waves are slowing down. You're almost asleep, in a light sleep, dreaming, or in deep hypnosis.

Delta

The slowest brain wave state. Your metabolic processes have slowed and you're in a deep sleep.

The alpha state is the best state for learning. In order to

Electrical activity in the brain fluctuates from high to low.

Brain Wave States:

Beta	Alert and active, thinking of many things at once
Alpha	Relaxed and alert, absorbing information
Theta	Almost asleep, dreaming to deep hypnosis
Delta	Deep sleep

quickly access a relaxed state every time you read, start by doing the following visualization:

Close your eyes and think of a place and time where you felt relaxed and at peace. It could be a favorite vacation spot or a special room at home. Picture yourself in this place and feel yourself relaxing. Do this for a few minutes to anchor this thought in your mind. You're now entering into an alpha brain wave state.

You should be able to return to this state quickly just by closing your eyes and thinking of the special place you pictured in the visualization. Try it again now.

Your brain takes cues from your body and the position you're in. To improve concentration, adopt a focused physiology. Sit up straight in your chair with both feet on the floor. Take a deep breath. Close your eyes. Think of your peaceful place. Roll your eyes up in your head; this puts you in a visual mode. Then open your eyes and look down at your book. Practice this a few times, so that you can go into alpha quickly. Remember to go through these steps every time you're about to read.

Now you have a positive attitude and new beliefs about your ability to read. You've committed yourself to being curious and know how to access a state of focused concentration. It's time to learn the eye and hand skills—the next step to becoming a Quantum Reader.

Step Three: Eye and Hand Skills

Following are several exercises to help you learn how to move your eyes in new ways across the page. Most of us read one word at a time. Our minds, however, can comprehend much more. The words have greater meaning for us when we see them together in groups because they are then in context. In order to see more than one word at once, we need to use our peripheral vision.

The alpha brain-wave state is the best state for learning.

To quickly access an alpha state:

Sit up

::

Take a deep breath

::

Close your eyes, think of your peaceful place

::

Roll your eyes up

::

Open your eyes and look down at your book

QUANTUM BUSINESS

To test your peripheral vision, put your arms straight out
in front of you with your hands in a fist, thumbs up. Slowly
move your hands out to each side, keeping your eyes
straight ahead. Stop your arms just before your thumbs get
out of view. Most people can see up to 45 degrees in each
direction from straight ahead, using only their peripheral
vision. If this is true for you, that means your range of
vision without moving your eyes is 90 degrees.

Here's another exercise: Look at the right-hand page.
Focus your eyes on the letter "A" in the center, and find
which letter you can see out to without moving your eyes.
Can you see out to "D," "G," or all the way to "J"? As you
practice Quantum Reading, your peripheral vision will
improve. Return to this exercise after you've practiced a
bit, and measure how much farther you can see.

Soft Focus

Focusing your eyes a different way can help you see
more words at once. One way is called "soft focus." Practice
soft focus by putting your attention on the white spaces
between the lines of text. As you read line by line, follow
the white space rather than the letters themselves. Let
your peripheral vision see the line above the white space.
This exercise expands your peripheral vision so you take
in more text at once. It also results in less eye fatigue.

Tri-Focus

This is a method of seeing groups of words instead of
single words. Imagine that each line of type is divided into
thirds, with the words clumped into three groups. As you
read, let your eyes jump from group to group instead of
from word to word, reading several words in a group at
once. To practice, look at the tri-focus exercise on page
209. Time yourself to see how much faster you read using

We use our peripheral vision to see more at one time.

```
J J J J J J J J J J J J J J J J J J J
J I I I I I I I I I I I I I I I I I J
J I H H H H H H H H H H H H H H I J
J I H G G G G G G G G G G G G H I J
J I H G F F F F F F F F F F G H I J
J I H G F E E E E E E E E F G H I J
J I H G F E D D D D D D E F G H I J
J I H G F E D C C C C D E F G H I J
J I H G F E D C B B B C D E F G H I J
J I H G F E D C B A B C D E F G H I J
J I H G F E D C B B B C D E F G H I J
J I H G F E D C C C C D E F G H I J
J I H G F E D D D D D D E F G H I J
J I H G F E E E E E E E E F G H I J
J I H G F F F F F F F F F F G H I J
J I H G G G G G G G G G G G G H I J
J I H H H H H H H H H H H H H H I J
J I I I I I I I I I I I I I I I I I J
J J J J J J J J J J J J J J J J J J J
```

this method. You can also practice this method anytime you like with an imaginary book. Close your eyes and move them left, center, right, repeatedly. Snap your fingers to the rhythm. Do this anytime you have a few minutes—when standing in line at the supermarket, sitting in the doctor's waiting room, or other similar situations.

Both soft focus and tri-focus exercises help you learn to read groups of words and develop your peripheral vision. It's going to take some practice to break the old habit of reading one word at a time, though; after all, you've probably been doing it since you learned to read. So stick with the new methods and they'll soon pay off.

Hand Skills

When you first learned to read, you ran your finger along the words to keep your place. Later you were told that this isn't the way "big people" read, and that it slows you down. Well, believe it or not, you're going to go back to using your finger again. And don't worry; studies have shown that this method of reading actually increases your speed. Using your finger or a pencil as a visual guide keeps you moving ahead and stops you from backtracking. Sometimes you may stop and reread words because you think you didn't get something, but if you're focused, you'll get it. You need to keep moving forward to increase your speed. As your eyes are "pushed" along by your finger, they move across the page faster and more efficiently. This is one of the most effective ways to speed up your reading. Even if you ignore other Quantum Reading skills, you can still double your speed, or more, with a visual guide to keep your eyes moving forward. You'll learn patterns for using a guide when you SuperScan and read the material. Right now, let's look at another hand skill, "page-turning."

TRI-Focus:
Practice reading several words together in a group.

The world, as a global
and is accelerating.
of students from diverse
from one another.
international SuperCamps
Forum we envisioned
parts of the world. At
going to happen, it felt
comes as a surprise
national programs
ging so fast, at times
remember distinctly the
phone call was a big
side of the world
into my office and
England who wants the
camp enrollment forms
minutes. We have a
dents attending our U.S.
world have become
porters. Our global
was written years ago,
priate than ever. An
tating a shift in
tive, responsible people
For change to happen
gether. Our international
In England, students
nationalities come
In Moscow, 1990, our
overwhelmed by the

community, has
I have experienced
cultures coming
This is the type of
provide. When we
SuperCamp pro-
that time we didn't
like a lofty goal.
that we arrived at
continue to expand.
it's challenging to
days when making
event, and sending
required weeks to
receive a phone call
address of someone
are being faxed to
growing number of
programs. People
good friends and
community is here
our company vision
international model
learning, resulting
participating in a
in the world, we
programs serve to
from a variety of
together with new
first international
generosity of the

gained momentum
firsthand the value
together to learn
opportunity our
started Learning
grams in many
know how this was
Today, it almost
our goal and inter-
The world is chan-
stay in step. I
a long distance
a letter to the other
arrive. Today I step
from a parent in
in New York, while
France, arriving in
international stu-
from around the
SuperCamp sup-
today. Although it
seems more appro-
of excellence, facili-
in educated, crea-
global community.
need to work to-
further this change.
backgrounds and
understanding.
program, we were
host families.

In order to Quantum Read you have to turn pages at Quantum speeds. To do this, sit at a table where you can support the book. Then hold onto the top center of the book with your left hand. Reach over with that same hand and turn the page from the top right corner. Use only your left hand to turn pages; when you're Quantum Reading, you'll be using your right hand as your visual guide. Practice page-turning for a few minutes. Time yourself to see how fast you can go. Fast page-turning improves your speed.

Step Four: SuperScan

Before you actually read a book, or any piece of reading, take time to SuperScan. It takes just a moment and will improve your speed and understanding, saving you time overall. When you SuperScan, you move at top speed, giving you an overview in just a few minutes. SuperScanning introduces you to the material so that when you return to speed-read it, you're already familiar with the contents. You'll be able to read even faster, and your comprehension will soar.

As you begin, be sure to prepare your reading area and use your ABCs, get into alpha state and remember to use your eye and hand skills. SuperScan involves several of the skills you've just learned—soft focus, page-turning, and using a visual guide. To SuperScan, use soft focus to take in the entire page at once. Using the finger on your right hand as a visual guide, let your finger "ski" back and forth down the page, like a skier slaloming down the slope. Do this first on the left-hand page, then on the right. Or, make a "U" pattern down the left and up the right page. These methods are called "ski" and "U."

Now we'll put your page-turning abilities to the test by combining them with your skiing or U-ing skills. Hold the book and turn pages with your left hand, and ski or "U"

Practice these movement patterns:

"Skiing"

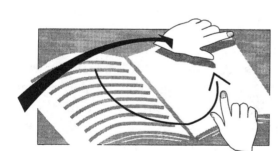

"U" Method

Practice skiing or U-ing as you also practice page-turning.

with your right. Practice skiing or U-ing and turning pages. See how fast you can go.

With most material, you will SuperScan several times before reading. First, quickly go through your book from cover to cover, looking for anything that stands out. As you SuperScan, talk to yourself about what you see in the book. Use the "C" of your ABCs—get curious and ask lots of questions. Say to yourself: "What is that? What does it mean? Now the author's talking about this—why?" When you re-read the material, your mind will pick out the answers.

Next, look for pictures and graphs. The third time around, scan titles, headings, and chapter summaries. On your final scan, look for important words and key phrases. When you finish scanning, begin a Mind Map about what you remember. Draw branches for any questions you want answered. (You will finish the Mind Map at the end of the Quantum Reading Process.)

SuperScan is like an eagle circling the sky in search of its prey. When an eagle first arrives at its hunting territory, it flies high in the sky to take in the whole terrain, noticing major features with its eagle eyes. After it has the overall picture, it flies slightly lower so it can pick up more detail. At this level, it can see where there are crags in the rocks, where the grass grows high, and the types of trees in the grove. The eagle then swoops even lower. Now he can see minute details in the landscape—buds on the trees, small burrows in the ground, and most important, his prey. Now, and only now does the eagle swoop down to the ground to snatch up a small field mouse with speed and precision.

You are a reading eagle. SuperScanning is like the eagle taking the first flight through its territory. You get the big picture and see all the terrain in the book. Like an eagle, you circle in search of answers to your questions. You move through the book several times, depending on the complexity of the terrain, beginning up high, looking at the big features and moving into more and more detail.

Step Five: Read

Now you're ready to dive into the material, homing in on the answers to questions you asked during SuperScan. As a reading eagle, you're swooping down to the ground to hunt down all the details you can grab. You do this by reading line by line, using your finger as a guide. Move your finger along the lines of text as you read this book. Your finger should move your eyes forward at a speed that is fast, just at the edge of your comfort level. Your eagle eyes should be just ahead of your finger. When you come to the end of a line, quickly move to the line below. Now push yourself to move a little faster. Use your peripheral vision to take in several words at once. With practice, you'll pick up speed and improve comprehension. As you build confidence for your fastest reading, you may want to ski down the page, taking in whole lines or paragraphs at once.

Step Six: Review

When you finish reading, complete your Mind Map. Keep your Mind Map folded in the front of your book. You can read it whenever you need a quick review of the main ideas in the book.

You may also want to try telling someone else about what you read, or talk to yourself. This will help you understand and remember the material.

Now that you have all the skills you need to be a Quantum Reader, let's go over the entire Quantum Reading Process.

Putting It All Together, Step by Step:
The Quantum Reading Process

Get out a book or other material you need to read and go through the entire process. Practice the process using different reading materials until you're comfortable with it.

Step One: Prepare
Prepare your reading area. Use your ABCs. Check your attitude and beliefs. Get curious! Ask questions.

Step Two: Get Into State
Concentrate fully by accessing alpha state. Sit up straight, breathe deeply, close your eyes, think of your peaceful place, roll your eyes up, then look down.

Step Three: Use Eye and Hand Skills
Remind yourself to use your eye and hand skills. Try soft focus and tri-focus. Concentrate on using peripheral vision to see groups of words at once. Hold the top of your book with your left hand, and use your right hand as a guide.

Step Four: SuperScan
Warm up with SuperScan. Use the "ski" or "U" method. Repeat the process as many times as necessary, depending on the difficulty of your reading material.

Step Five: Read
Go back and read the material you just SuperScanned. Remember to stay in alpha state. If you lose focus, stop and get back into state by going through Step Two again. Use your eye and hand skills. See groups of words, and use a visual guide. Also, you may want to take time to add to your Mind Map, and underline or highlight as you read.

Step Six: Review

The Quantum Reading Process

Follow these steps:

 1   Prepare

 2   Get into State

 3   Use Eye and Hand Skills

 4   SuperScan

  5   Read

 6   Review

Take time to complete your Mind Map and talk about what you've read.

See the diagram on the right-hand page for a visual review. This will help you remember the steps. The top half represents steps one through four, the skills you need to practice repeatedly to improve your reading. This is the circling eagle, getting the big picture, asking questions, and moving in ever closer. During steps five and six (read and review), the eagle dives in and attacks the material, picking out key information.

Now that you've learned the Quantum Reading Process, repeat the first exercise you did when you timed your initial reading speed. Continue where you left off in *The Einstein Factor* and see how your reading speed has increased. Then celebrate your achievement!

Tips

Decide how much you're going to read before you begin. Most of us have experienced stopping in the middle of our reading to see how much farther we have to go. Get this over with before you start. Decide how much you'll read, then mark the spot with a bookmark. This simple step will free you to concentrate on your reading.

If you have a large stack of books to catch up on, choose four or five and concentrate on those for a month. Practice by SuperScanning a book for a few days or a week. Then read and Mind Map it. Rotate in a new book each week. After SuperScanning, reading, and Mind Mapping, you'll know the material extensively and your Mind Map will serve as a review whenever needed. You'll also get through that stack a lot faster then you ever expected.

If you did the exercises in this chapter, you've already done a lot to improve your reading. Keep working on

Practice steps 1–4 several times before moving to steps 5 & 6.

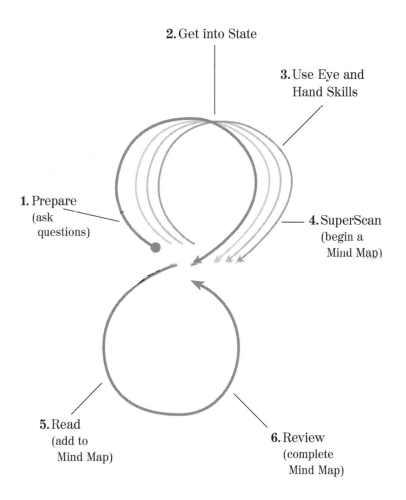

2. Get into State

3. Use Eye and Hand Skills

1. Prepare (ask questions)

4. SuperScan (begin a Mind Map)

5. Read (add to Mind Map)

6. Review (complete Mind Map)

increasing your speed and comprehension. I recommend practicing steps one through four (the circling eagle), for five minutes a day. Think of the time you'll save and the possibilities that lie ahead.

Congratulations! Now you're a Quantum Reader.

Celebrate Your Learning!

! *What are three key ways that increase speed and comprehension?*

- High interest
- Focused concentration
- Using techniques employing both hemispheres of the brain

! *Why is an alpha brain wave state beneficial for reading?*

It is a relaxed, yet comfortable state for improved concentration.

! *How can you increase your peripheral vision?*

By practicing "soft focus"—focusing on the white space between the lines and the "tri-focus" exercise—focusing on groups of words.

! *What one thing can you do that will double your reading speed?*

Use a visual guide. It stops you from backtracking. For most effective reading, use the six-step Quantum Reading Process.

11

Finding Value
In Failure

 *What's the difference between
the internal and the external
consequences of failure?*

 *How can you control the internal
consequences of your failures?*

 *How do you overcome your
fear of failure?*

 *What can you do to help yourself
succeed more often?*

When you hear the word "failure," what do you think? Bad report cards, losing a job, a marriage gone sour? "Failure" is a label we tend to stick on any unsuccessful venture, and once applied, it brands us incompetent, discouraging us from future attempts at success.

Early in life, failure has little meaning, if any. As children, we had no concept of failure. If we had, we'd never have learned to walk, talk, and conquer all the other obstacles life threw at us.

If you didn't succeed at your first attempts to catch a ball or swing a bat, you didn't say, "Well, I'm a failure at baseball," and give up the game. No, you just kept chasing after the ball and swinging the bat until your mother called you in for dinner. In grade school, if you got a poor grade on one math test, you probably didn't call yourself a math failure and quit trying. In fact, for the first five to ten years of your life, you were probably so motivated to learn new things that you just kept going in spite of any setbacks.

But somewhere along the way, someone—your parents, a teacher, a coach—someone whose opinion you valued, taught you that trying something and not succeeding was bad. You heard people labeled as "failures" and you got the message this was to be avoided. Before long, you developed a fear of failure—and the damage was done.

Because society views failure in such a negative way, many of us simply avoid trying new things rather than risk failure. Instead, we stick with what we know: predictable responses, practiced skills, things that are familiar, and comfortable. This is known as the "comfort zone," and staying within our comfort zone can stop us from trying new things, thereby saving us from suffering the "humiliation" of failure. But it can also cost us opportunities.

Failure is something we learn to fear as we grow older.

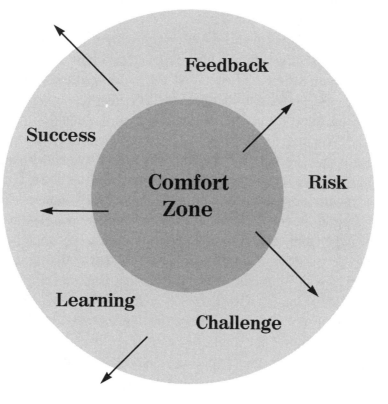

Fear of failure keeps us in our comfort zone.

What It Means to Fail

Let's take a closer look at what it means to fail. When we fail at something, we face two types of consequences—external and internal. External consequences are what happen out in the world. For example, in school, if you don't understand math and do poorly at it, the consequence is a low grade. Later in life, if you apply for a job and it goes to someone else, the consequence is you don't get that particular job. These things affect you, but essentially, they happen outside of you.

Internal consequences reflect the emotional side of failure—what you think about yourself and how you interpret your actions. If you didn't get a passing grade on a math test, you might say to yourself, "I failed the math test. I'm an idiot. I'll never understand it, why should I even try?" You may even go on to feel sorry for yourself, avoid math, and become fearful and threatened whenever you have to take a math test. You've interpreted one low grade to mean a low IQ and a lifetime of failure with numbers.

Getting passed over for a new job is an emotional situation; you may feel you put yourself on the spot by applying for the position in the first place. You may tell yourself, "What was I thinking, applying for that position? I could never get that job with today's competition. I'm embarrassed I even tried. Now I have to tell everyone I didn't get the job. I'll look like a real loser."

In both situations, what you think about the failure—not the real, external result—is what makes it a negative experience.

Let's look at both situations objectively as a disinterested observer might. Viewed objectively, a low grade on a test means only that you didn't understand the information; you need help with the concepts. It doesn't mean you're

Often external consequences of a situation are small, while internal consequences are what's harmful.

Failure produces two consequences:

External – What happens out in the world

Internal – What you think about yourself and how you interpret your actions mentally deficient or that you will never understand. It just means you need help.

Not getting the job means they picked someone else, that's all. It doesn't mean the other person is better than you, or that you aren't capable. In the external world, the world outside your own mind, you didn't lose anything by applying for the job. The point is, there's no way you could have gotten it if you'd never applied.

Often the external consequences of a situation are small or even nonexistent, while the internal consequences— worrying about what others will think if you fail—can be harmful. These feelings can become so powerful that they stop you from even trying. It's true that if you don't try you won't fail . . . but you won't succeed, either. Worse yet, you won't even have the opportunity to succeed—not a chance.

Change Your Thinking, Change Your Life

Luckily, you can control your internal consequences simply by changing the way you think. Back in the 1980's, the inspirational speaker Terry Cole-Whittaker wrote a book whose title is a valuable message in itself. It's called, *What You Think of Me Is None of My Business*. That's a good motto to live by. Looking at things objectively and having a little confidence in yourself can get you past any imagined failures.

After 13 years of schooling, my sister, Jean Forman, graduated from medical school near the top of her class and completed her residency with flying colors. A tremendous achievement, especially when you consider she was 53 years old at the time. But with all that, she still lacked confidence in her abilities. She did so well in school that a university contacted her and invited her to join their research team.

As the interviewer reviewed her file, she nervously asked, "Why did you pick me? You don't even know me."

"Oh, yes we do," he replied. "You're highly skilled, inquisitive, and intelligent, and we also know you have very little confidence in your doctoring. The skill, the inquisitiveness, the intelligence—those we can't help you with. Those are the gifts you bring to this organization. But the confidence, that we can give you. That's no problem."

The interviewer realized my sister's fear of failure might block her from accepting the job, and he wanted to defuse that fear right on the spot.

Rick Miller, AT&T's chief financial officer, believes that true success is giving it your best shot, regardless of the final results. He maintains that if you can look in the mirror and say "I did my best," no matter what the outcome, that's success.

The worst part of having negative feelings about your abilities is that it can become a habit, and habits are comfortable. It's easier to say "I can't" than to admit you're afraid to try. Your responses become automatic: "That's too hard." "I'm burned out." "I don't have enough time." "I can't afford it." You become boxed in by your comfort zone. The only way to break out is to abolish the negative, debilitating thoughts and start thinking positively.

Learning Won't Happen in an Atmosphere of Fear

When we break out of our comfort zones, we can accomplish great things. So why are we afraid to risk making a mistake when we can gain so much just by trying? The answer is fear. As we learned from Dr. W. Edwards Deming in Chapter 3, fear is the number-one problem in the workplace. It keeps people from trying new ideas, and if they don't try, they can't possibly improve.

QUANTUM BUSINESS

Many of us are reluctant to try new things at work. Maybe we fear a tyrannical boss will verbally abuse us, or worse, we might be demoted or lose our job. We may even believe that a poor decision on our part will destroy the entire company. Most often, these thoughts are way out of proportion to the actual situation. If we stop and look at things objectively, and focus on the real, external consequences, we can gather the courage to take action.

If fear is indeed the number-one problem in the workplace, the best solution is for businesses to actively look for ways to eliminate fear and instead build an atmosphere of trust. In a fearful environment, many valuable things never happen. Employees don't ask questions, don't get the help they need to do a better job, don't practice their skills, don't communicate their ideas or concerns, and don't receive constructive feedback. Because they're human, though, they still make mistakes. So in an atmosphere of fear, improvement is stifled while mistakes live on.

Throughout this book, we've discussed the importance of a positive work environment. A trusting, open environment can make all the difference in a company's productivity, effectiveness, and ultimate success. In a trusting environment, everyone participates more and accomplishes more. They ask questions, voice their opinions, and receive input from others. Trusting others allows each person to accomplish things they never thought they could do—and might not have been able to do on their own. Plus, they feel good about themselves. Success leads to even greater participation. The greater the participation, the more they accomplish and the more joy they find in their work.

Failure Leads to Success

You may be thinking, All this sounds great, but how do I

overcome my fear of failure? Here's how: Think of "failure" as "feedback." See failures as events that provide information you need to make adjustments in your actions, and these adjustments will lead to your success.

When things don't work out, ask yourself, What have I learned from this experience? What value can I find in it? What will I do differently next time? Mistakes are opportunities for learning. Oscar Wilde said, "Experience . . . is simply the name we give to our mistakes." The only real failure is not learning from your mistakes.

Before you read on, think about the previous sentence: The only real failure is not learning from your mistakes. Striking out is not a failure. Striking out on the same kind of pitch from the same pitcher in your next time up, that's failure. But even the second strike-out is an opportunity to learn. Even the best realize they're constantly making mistakes. They constantly learn from those mistakes so as to avoid making them again.

Pete Rose got more hits in his career than any man in over 100 years of major league history. When he didn't swing at a pitch, he made a habit of watching the ball go past him and into the catcher's mitt. Almost nobody does that. Most hitters just watch the ball cross the plate and wait for the umpire's call.

Somebody once asked Rose why he watched the ball until it was caught. His reply: "I want to see what that pitch does—whether it drops or curves, whether it ends up being called a strike or a ball, and why. That way, if it's a strike, the next time I'll know I shouldn't let that pitch go. Next time, I'll swing at it."

Rose also liked to go to the plate with a clean black bat. Why? Because when he hit the ball, it would leave a visible mark, and later he could examine the mark and know how

QUANTUM BUSINESS

much he was off in his swing. He could make an adjustment, and next time hit the ball more solidly. Is it any wonder he got over 4,000 hits? While other players would strike out, throw the bat down, and curse their mistakes, Pete Rose was constantly learning from his.

Most highly successful business people got where they are after making a few mistakes—even when the mistakes were whoppers. Remember the infamous "New Coke" fiasco when the company launched a new product in an effort to combat Pepsi's growing popularity and reverse Coca-Cola's 20-year market share decline? The man responsible for this historic blunder was Sergio Zyman, Coca-Cola's marketing "genius." Despite the extensive market research he conducted, the thousands of taste tests, the careful test marketing—when New Coke came out, fans of the old Coke were incensed. They didn't care for the new product at all. After faltering sales, the product was removed from the shelves and replaced by "Coke Classic," which is nothing more than old Coke relabeled.

Zyman left Coca-Cola in disgrace a year after the incident. But he began his own consulting business and developed it into a profitable venture. A few years later, surprisingly, Coca-Cola wooed him back. Why on earth would a company want to rehire someone who made the biggest mistake in a hundred years of its history? Management felt it was the company's reluctance to tolerate mistakes that had made it noncompetitive. They had come to understand that if the main motivator behind something is the avoidance of failure, the result will be inactivity.

In the end, the company found success in the New Coke failure. When old Coke returned to the market, the company experienced its biggest-ever surge in sales, not

Most highly successful business people got where they are after making a few mistakes.

Even when the mistakes were whoppers!

only reversing the market share decline, but propelling it to even greater dominance. With that kind of result, some executives have joked, the company should make mistakes like that more often.

Learn from Every Failure and Every Success

Think of both failures and successes as learning experiences. In each case, ask yourself what you learned and what you'll do differently next time. Then do your homework. "Life is a series of outcomes," says Simone Caruthers, a psychologist and business consultant. "Sometimes the outcome is what you want. Great. Figure out what you did right. Sometimes the outcome is what you don't want. Great. Figure out what you did so you don't do it again."

Many businesses are beginning to recognize the value of failure as a learning experience. Harvard Business School professor John Kotter says that in the past a job candidate who had experienced a big failure wouldn't stand much of a chance of getting the job. But today companies look at candidates differently. In fact, many are reluctant to hire someone who has never failed. Failure shows a willingness to take risks and try new ideas—valuable skills in today's rapidly changing business environment.

Tommy Lasorda, the much-quoted former manager of the Los Angeles Dodgers once said, "The only trouble with success is that it doesn't teach you how to deal with failure." As someone who's had a lot of both, he knows what he's talking about.

In my life, my most difficult failures gave birth to my greatest successes. When I lost all my money, other people's money, and the Burklyn Business School due to bad investments, I faced one of the most difficult times of my life. But I also learned to listen to my gut feelings and trust myself, instead of thinking that others must know better and blindly following them. Also, I learned that the end does not justify the means, as the old saying claims. I tried to tell myself that since the money was going toward the good work we were doing at Burklyn, it was okay to gamble with stock options, something I knew little about. Now I stay away from anything that isn't aligned with my values and interests.

Like failures, successes are also opportunities to learn. Examine each success, and question what specifically made it successful.

Recognize that everything you do is a learning experience and see failure as an opportunity to learn and grow. The most successful executives seem unacquainted with the concept of failure. Instead, they see failures as "false starts," merely stumbles on the steps to greatness.

Reward Yourself

Give yourself some kind of reward for each step you take toward a goal. Instead of focusing on mistakes, acknowledge your successes. When you finally reach your goal, celebrate! Share your accomplishment with others. The celebration is a conscious way of letting go of any frustrations or feelings of failure or inadequacy that you may have held along the way. Take pride in your achievements—your strengthened confidence will lead you toward new ventures and greater achievements.

If I had to choose one idea about failure that I feel would do you the most good, it would be this: Look upon it as a gift. Look upon failure as something valuable that has been given to you to help you learn, and grow, and adjust so that in your next attempt, you'll be closer to getting the result you want. If you look at failure in this way, you'll never see it as final, or fatal. Rather than being discouraged by an unsuccessful result, you'll be encouraged and energized. You'll welcome failure, rather than dread it. You'll never again let the fear of failure keep you from trying. And most important, you'll see every failure as just another step on the road to your inevitable success.

Celebrate Your Learning!

! *What's the difference between the internal and external consequences of failure?*

External consequences are the results of failure that happen out in the world. Internal consequences are what you think of yourself and how you interpret your failures.

! *How can you control the internal consequences of your failures?*

Simply by changing the way you think.

! *How do you overcome your fear of failure?*

Think of failure as "feedback." See failures as events that provide information you need to make changes and adjustments in your actions, and that these adjustments will lead to your success.

! *What can you do to help yourself succeed more often?*

- See things from the perspective of the customer or employee.
- Stay alert to changes in trends and what the competition is doing.
- Create a supportive environment.
- Learn from every failure and every success.
- Reward yourself for each successful step.

12

Working Magic with Your Memory

 Why is having a strong WIIFM especially important to memory?

 Which two skills are the basis of memory skills?

 What elements make information more memorable?

 How can you remember names more easily?

QUANTUM BUSINESS

D.o you remember people's faces but not their names? Have you ever wished you could make your speeches more spontaneous-sounding and not have to constantly refer to your notes? Memory skills are important both for business and personal success, and through the years, experts have produced numerous books, tapes, and seminars about how to improve your memory. But just how well do these methods work? Will you even remember how to use them once you've completed the book or seminar? More importantly, will you be motivated to use them? And will knowing and using the skills have a significant impact on your life?

This chapter explains core memory skills—those that make the most difference. All the memory classes in the world won't help you in the least if what they teach doesn't fit your style. You must see the value in the skills and actually be excited about them before you'll use them.

So, first you need to discover the WIIFM. How can you benefit from a better memory? Eric Jensen, author of *The Learning Brain* (Turning Point Publishing, San Diego, 1994), makes the point that we learn and remember those things that are important to our survival—not only our physical survival, but also our perceived emotional survival, professional survival, and survival in personal relationships. If I believe I need to master new technology to stay in business, I'm motivated to learn about it.

As I mentioned in Chapter 4, Larry Squire, a neuropsychologist at the University of California, San Diego, has done an exploration of those components of the brain that process memory and learning. He found that the hippocampus, located in the forebrain, plays a crucial role in cataloging memories. It temporarily records events, then helps store the information in long-term memory. Robert

Sylwester, a college professor and researcher at the University of Oregon, believes the hippocampus acts like a librarian, weighing information, cataloging it, and filing it away. If it determines the information is valuable, it helps place it in long-term storage in the neocortex. If Sylwester's research is true, it's a powerful validation of the importance of discovering the WIIFM. Without the WIIFM, the hippocampus never recognizes the importance of certain information, and therefore never helps place that information in long-term memory.

Improve Your Memory for Fun and Profit

Picture yourself enjoying the benefits of a powerful memory. Imagine all the ways you might use it to increase your effectiveness each day.

- You're in the middle of having to tell an employee he made a major mistake, when suddenly you remember some tips from a management book you recently read. You quickly switch to these tested, empowering communication skills and both you and the employee feel better after the talk.

- The book sitting on your nightstand is one you've been wanting to read for ages, but you haven't had the time. Next time you see it, you remember the specific steps in the Quantum Reading Process you learned earlier in this book.

- You have to give a presentation, but instead of practically reading your prepared speech word for word, you remember a method you learned for easily recalling your main points . . . in order.

- You're at an important meeting with new clients, and

you're able to recall the strategies you learned for remembering the name of every person there. In fact, even before you got to the meeting, you had memorized the names and positions of each person so that you were able to quickly and effortlessly put the names with the faces.

What Would These Skills Do for Your Career?

Your job isn't the only situation in which you can use good memory skills, though. It's also fun, not to mention convenient, to memorize numbers such as your driver's license, license plate, passport, bank account, PIN, and locker combination. Remembering important phone numbers and dates, like birthdays and anniversaries, can make your life easier and less stressful. Most people know their Social Security number, but how many know their spouse's number? Just last week I was asked for my husband Joe's number on a form I was filling out. I was able to write it from memory, saving the time and trouble of looking it up.

My son Grant first got me excited about the possibilities of memory skills. He learned the skills at the first SuperCamp in 1982 and uses them more consistently than anyone I know. In high school, his memory skills helped him increase his score on the SAT. He used them to learn 1,600 vocabulary words in one weekend, increasing his verbal score from the 66th percentile to the 99th.

Memory skills also helped Grant get his master's degree in business administration, and he still considers them a valuable tool in his career. As manager of Harry Caray's restaurant in Chicago, he memorized the names of his 165 employees his first week on the job. Then, during a long airplane trip, he memorized over 1,000 food and beverage

Memory skills are valuable in your career and personal life.

Memory is the stepping-stone to thinking, because without remembering facts, you cannot think, conceptualize, reason, make decisions, create, or contribute.

HARRY LORAYNE

It's fun and convenient to memorize:

Phone numbers

::

Important dates

::

Driver's license and Social Security numbers

::

Names

::

Sales figures and marketing statistics

::

To-do lists

::

Computer codes, formulas, equations

items along with their assigned accounting numbers. He also uses his memory skills to greatly increase his Spanish vocabulary so that he can communicate with the Spanish-speaking members of his staff. And the list goes on. Throughout every day, he builds on and discovers more uses for memory skills.

The best thing about these memory skills is they're fun to practice. And it's even more fun to amaze your colleagues, friends, and yourself with your expertise. When Grant and I are riding in a car together, he'll quiz me: "Tell me the code for remembering that license plate. Name all the U.S. presidents, in order."

Years ago when I was in real estate, I experienced my first successes with memory systems. The weekend before taking the real estate broker's exam, I took a cram course that included a presentation by memory expert Arthur Bornstein. In the five days following the class, I was able to memorize 40 pages of notes, word for word. On test day, I knew the answers and passed the exam. Then I found many other uses for effective memory skills. Since I was working in San Francisco, I memorized the street names from one end of the city to the other. I spent a lot of time each day driving, and this kept me occupied, as I could practice and test myself as I drove.

I had a strong incentive to learn all of these things. They were necessary for professional survival, at least at some level of consciousness. So, I had a strong WIIFM to learn them.

The first step toward developing memory skills you'll actually use is to start with a commitment. Commit to spending a week practicing these strategies. After a week, they'll come to you effortlessly and will be yours for life.

What We Remember Most

Our chances of remembering are best when the information includes more than one of the following eight elements: sensory, intense, emotional, outstanding, survival, personal importance, repetition, and firsts and lasts.

To create the strongest associations, focus on the eight following words and what they stand for:

1. Sensory

It may sound simplistic, but the first skill you need to learn is simply to pay attention. Why? Because it's difficult to remember something when you aren't paying attention in the first place.

Using a combination of sight, sound, motion, smell, and taste creates the strongest memories. Focus on these elements:

Sights — Use color and tones, bright and dark. Explore details. Take enough time to see things clearly in your mind.

Sounds — Hear the sound of something whenever possible. Practice listening attentively.

Motion — See the items moving together. Also, move as you talk. In giving a speech, if I can't remember the next thing I'm planning to say, it sometimes helps to start walking across the stage; then it comes to me.

Feel — Remembering through touch can also be powerful. Do you remember any phone numbers by physically starting to dial them, feeling the buttons and recreating the pattern? If someone asks you for the number, you may find it difficult to recall

without imagining to dial a phone. Also
retracing our steps helps us remember our
thoughts, such as where we left something
we're trying to find.

Smells — Imagine the fragrance. Smell often triggers more than facts. The emotions and
tone of an event can be relived through a
powerful olfactory association.

Taste — Imagine what something tastes like,
especially strong tastes like lemon
or coffee.

Recent brain theory supports the importance of using all
of your senses. For the strongest recall, use as many of the
above senses as possible, and in different combinations.
Researchers have learned that memory of an object isn't
stored whole, but remains where it was when it was first
perceived. Dr. Nina Dronkers, of the VA Northern
California Health Care System and the University of
California at Davis, noted that when we think of a tree, "We
know the sound it makes in the wind, the look of the trunk,
the shape of a leaf." Each of these details may come from a
different place in the brain. "The idea that knowledge is
distributed is gaining wide acceptance," according to
Dronkers.

New research, as reported in a *New York Times* piece
titled "The Brain's Memory System Comes into Focus," by
Philip J. Hilts, finds that the brain is an indexer, organizing
information into categories. It breaks information down
into components, and stores each separately. When you
recall a creature such as a horse—the texture of its hair, the
fact it can run fast, its smell, the sound it makes, and so on—
the brain stores these bits of information separately.

Pay attention!
It's difficult to remember something when you aren't paying attention in the first place.

 Observe details

 Listen attentively

 Move your body

 Touch things

 Take in smells

 Be aware of taste

Another part of the brain takes this information and merges the facts together so that we recognize the whole picture. However this complete picture is not stored permanently.

Dr. Antonio R. Damasio, author of *Descartes' Error* (Putnam, New York, 1994), created the notion of "convergence zones," or indexes that draw information from elsewhere in the brain. Damasio says these brain indexes do not contain the memories themselves, only the instructions on how to rekindle many related features and memories associated with them.

This explains why it's so important to layer our associations with strong visual images, sounds, smells, touch, and motion.

2. Intense

To make your images memorable, make them intense: absurd, sexual, colorful, exaggerated, and imaginative. For example:

Imaginative sights	— An enormous fly, a tiny elephant, vibrant colors.
Absurd sounds	— Your boss talking like Donald Duck.
Exaggerated movements	— In the old Disney "Flubber" movies, basketball players could jump high above the baskets.

Even though they're intense, be sure to keep your images positive. The mind wants to forget negative and harmful images, so keeping them positive makes them more memorable. If you visualize hitting another person, it should be done in a playful slapstick style. Avoid harmful intent.

Knowledge is distributed. Details come from different places in the brain.

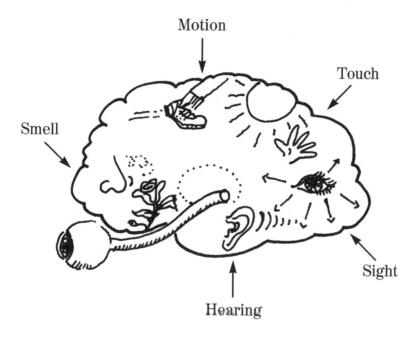

Inspired by A. Damasio and H. Damasio,
Scientific American, September, 1992.

*"Convergence" zones draw information together
to make complete images.*

3. Outstanding

Use different qualities, such as all people wearing brown except one person wearing blue. It's not really intense, just different.

4. Emotional

Images charged with love, happiness, and sorrow are easy to remember. Using images of warm feelings, the feelings that make your heart race and bring a glow of happiness, will help your memory and your outlook.

5. Survival

As I mentioned at the beginning of the chapter, a strong WIIFM that's tied to your survival in some area increases your motivation to remember.

6. Personal Importance

Use associations personal to your life such as members of your family, your home, office, friends, events, and things that are special to you.

7. Repetition

Many of us study by repeating something over and over. Some information sticks for a short time, perhaps long enough for us to pass an exam or give a presentation, but we even forget most of that as time passes. Another, more effective way to use repetition is to focus intently on the material and repeat it in different ways, such as saying it out loud and making a Mind Map. Research shows that recall greatly improves if we review information within 24 hours, again in 48 hours, and then in seven days. From then on, with only infrequent reviews, you'll be able to recall the information easily.

8. First and Last

If you were to read a list of items, you'd most likely remember the first thing on the list and the last. When you're introduced to a new group of people, you usually remember best the names of the person you met first and the one you met last. I find, for example, that the opening and closing of a movie will stick in my mind, but I often forget the middle.

To improve your memory, create more firsts and lasts by breaking down information into many small chunks. When you're studying or trying to learn something new, take short, frequent breaks—at least every 30 minutes. This helps you retain more information.

Now you've learned the eight ways people tend to remember best. But how do you remember them? We all know the characters from the movie "The Wizard of Oz": Dorothy, the Wicked Witch, Scarecrow, Tin Man, Cowardly Lion, the Wizard, the Guards, and Auntie Em and Uncle Henry. I will show you how each of these characters may represent one of the eight elements.

1. Sensory

Think of Dorothy as we remember the movie through her eyes. We start by seeing it in black and white—then it switches to color. Imagine what Dorothy sees, hears, smells, and feels.

2. Intense

The Wicked Witch certainly used intense words and motions. Imagine her swirling through the sky, and yelling in her cackly voice.

3. Outstanding

Think of the Scarecrow. He certainly stood out from the other scarecrows. See him moving and talking.

4. Emotional

Picture the Tin Man yearning for a heart. Then see his huge red heart and hear it pounding.

5. Survival

Picture the Cowardly Lion looking for courage so he could survive in the world. See him quivering with fear.

6. Personal Importance

The Wizard certainly made himself important in the Emerald City.

7. Repetition

Think of the Guards who were always saying, "Oh-ee-oh. Oh, oh," over and over. Hear the tune from the movie.

8. First and Last

Auntie Em and Uncle Henry only appear at the beginning and the end of the movie. See them worried at the beginning and happy at the end.

Take a moment to review these. Then close your eyes and say the eight elements for a strong memory.

Memory Methods—Imagination and Association

To succeed in remembering, you need to develop a strong, clear, vivid imagination and learn to make strong, clear, vivid associations.

Imagination is the ability to see, hear, and sense things in your mind—to create scenes and pictures, both still and moving. For example, picture someplace you know, such as your kitchen. With your eyes open or closed, can you see in your mind what sits on the counter? Where you keep your drinking glasses? Can you picture yourself washing a glass? Or see it dropping and hear it shattering on the floor? Now imagine something you've never seen, like a zebra with orange and green stripes or a dog flying like a

Associate the "Easy Eight" with characters from "The Wizard of Oz".

Dorothy

Sensory

We experience
the movie through her

Wicked Witch

Intense

She uses intense
words and motions

Scarecrow

Outstanding

Being distinct from
the others

Tin Man

Emotional

He yearns for a heart

Cowardly Lion

Survival

He's looking for
courage to survive

Wizard

Personal Importance

He made himself
important

The Guards

Repetition

Repetitive in their
musical chants

**Auntie Em and
Uncle Henry**

First and Last

They appear at the
beginning/end of movie

bird. Can you see it? That's imagination.

Association is the ability to take one familiar object and connect it with something you're trying to remember. We associate information with sight, sound, smell, and touch. We choose those things most obvious to us personally—the strongest association that comes to mind. No matter what type of association you use, it's important to discover your strongest area—that is, whether you tend to be more visual, auditory, or kinesthetic.

For most people, the strongest associations are visual. For example, if you wanted to associate objects with numbers, such as the number one and a tree, you could picture the tree trunk as a large number one. To associate the number three with a foot you could picture the three turned sideways. It might look like the toes on your foot. To remember two objects, such as a tree and a chair, you could picture a chair rocking on top of a tree, or a tree growing out of the center of the chair. Get the picture?

To reinforce an image, we can use more than one of our senses. See a picture of a tree, hear the wind through its branches, smell the sweet smells of the blossoms, and feel the texture of its trunk against your skin.

These examples show how you can use associations to memorize concrete things—the stuff you can see, hear, smell, and touch. Other things may not be so obvious. You may even need to invent an association.

We can also combine sounds with visual images to create associations. Take a word such as "prepare" and hear that "pare" sounds like "pear." Then fit the visual of a pear into your association. In this case, remember to hear the sound of syllables rather than seeing how the words are spelled.

At SuperCamp we teach students to remember things by having them act them out in some small way, creating a movement to go along with what they're trying to remember. For example, the motion for "clear vision" might be moving their hands like a windshield wiper. To "cement a point," they might stamp their feet. We'll teach a list of items, such as U.S. presidents or the mineral hardness scale, through movement, and if students get stuck on an item, we'll say, "Move your body." Even if they don't remember the exact motion, just the act of starting to move their bodies often brings the item to mind.

Linking

Linking is the next most basic memory skill. You can use it to memorize a list by associating each item on the list with the next. It can also be the foundation for other memory strategies. You link things you want to remember and string them together, associating one with another, with another.

As an example, here's an easy way to remember the zodiac signs. See a <u>ram</u> (Aries) butting heads with a <u>bull</u> (Taurus). On the bull's back are <u>twins</u> (Gemini), holding a <u>crab</u> (Cancer) because they want to eat it for dinner. The crab is pinching a <u>lion</u>'s (Leo) tail, which causes the lion to roar and break loose. The lion tries attacking a <u>virgin</u> (Virgo), who hits the lion with <u>scales</u> (Libra). She then throws the scales into a patch of <u>scorpions</u> (Scorpio), which get angered and try stinging an <u>archer</u> (Sagittarius), who escapes by jumping on the back of a <u>goat</u> (Capricorn). The goat runs into <u>water</u> (Aquarius), which is filled to overflow capacity with <u>fish</u> (Pisces), which jump out of the water onto the bank where the ram squashes them while butting heads with the bull, and on and on.

Notice the signs are in order. You probably already know your month and sign and can go forward or backward in the story from there.

QUANTUM   BUSINESS

Location

Location means associating items sequentially (in order) with specific locations. For example, you can associate a list of items with the parts of your body, starting with the top of your head, then your eyes, nose, mouth, chin, neck, shoulders, and on down to your feet. You can also use the face of a clock and associate things: one item with one o'clock, another with two o'clock, and so on.

One of my favorite location tricks is to associate items with things in my home. To use your home, always imagine the things in your home in the same order as you associate them with items you wish to remember. The order I always use is: the chalkboard hanging on my front door, a light switch just inside the door, the entry floor, the living room ceiling, and so on around my home. I use this method most often when I'm giving a speech. As I'm talking to the audience, I can actually visualize myself walking through the rooms, remembering items I want to cover by the area of my home with which I have associated them.

I imagine my introduction with key words written on the chalkboard. Then I picture the first two points with the two positions of the light switch. I see what I want to say next on the entry floor, and I move on through the entire speech that way. For me this method is very effective; I always know where I am in the speech and what comes next because I can see myself in each room. I suggest you come up with your own list of items using your own home or office. Be sure it's a place you know well and can easily picture in your mind. Attach items in your home to the numbers 1 through 20, in the order you would see these items as you walk through your home. Use the floor plan on the page to the right to help you get started.

Create a list of 20 items that you see as you move through your home.

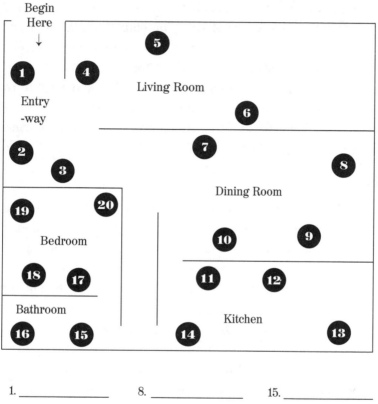

1. _____   8. _____   15. _____

2. _____   9. _____   16. _____

3. _____   10. _____   17. _____

4. _____   11. _____   18. _____

5. _____   12. _____   19. _____

6. _____   13. _____   20. _____

7. _____   14. _____

Acronyms

Acronyms take the first letter of several words and create another word. An acronym you might remember from your school days is **HOMES**, which helps students remember the names of the Great Lakes: Huron, Ontario, Michigan, Erie, and Superior.

In writing, we teach **MAPS**, or sometimes **SPAM** for fun, to remember tools for writing more descriptively. Metaphor, Alliteration, Personification, and Simile.

We sometimes even make up a word, like **FRAKAA**, to remember principles of a learning organization. Foundation, Relationships, Acquire Knowledge, Action, and Acknowledge.

Cues

We've all heard the old-fashioned idea of tying a string around our finger to remind us of something—this is a cue, and it's not really all that out of date. A cue can be anything that triggers you to remember something. When I find myself rushing out of the office and don't have time to scribble down a note, I'll put something conspicuously out of place on my desk, like placing my phone right in the center. When I come in the next morning, the phone reminds me of what I needed to remember. This is a cue.

Sometimes just beginning a known phrase can help us remember something. A friend of mine was recently trying to remember the name of the Beaver's big brother on the old "Leave It to Beaver" television show. In her mind, she could hear Beaver saying, "Gee, _____. I don't know." But she couldn't fill in the blank with the brother's name. Finally, she said the phrase over and over, trying different names until the name "Wally" popped into her mind. That was it! "Gee, Wally. I don't know."

Acronyms are useful memory tools.

Take the first letter of several words and create another word as in:

- **M**others
- **A**gainst
- **D**runk
- **D**rivers

or make up a word, such as **FRAKAA**

- **F**oundation
- **R**elationships
- **A**cquire
  Knowlege
- **A**ction
- **A**cknowledge

Rote

Repeating something over and over is probably the least effective way to remember something, but it does work for short-term memorization. You probably used this method yourself while in school to study for a test.

Memorizing Quantum Business

Here are some examples of memory techniques you can use to remember things I've covered in the book:

Memorizing the 8 Keys of Excellence

Use your body by associating each key to a specific body part.

1. **Eyes**	Integrity	By looking into your eyes, people can see you have great integrity. They also see huge bright "I's" in your eyes.
2. **Nose**	Failure Leads to Success	You can smell success with your nose.
3. **Mouth**	Speak with Good Purpose	You speak through your mouth and only with good purpose.
4. **Chin**	This Is It	Always walk with your chin up and have a great attitude about all you do.

To memorize the 8 Keys of Excellence, use your body to associate specific keys with body parts.

Integrity

Failure Leads
to Success

Speak with
Good Purpose

This Is It

Commitment

Ownership

Flexibility

Balance

5. **Arms**	Commitment	I flex my muscles to show I'm strong and committed.
6. **Stomach**	Ownership	I am what I eat and I take ownership of who I am and of my actions.
7. **Legs**	Flexibility	As I'm highly flexible, my legs can do amazing feats. I'm open to new ideas and changes.
8. **Feet**	Balance	I'm balanced on my feet. My life is about keeping balance in all areas of my life.

The Quantum Reading Process

One way you can remember the Quantum Reading Process is by associating it with major holidays. This list includes the U.S. and Christian holidays that most Americans celebrate. You can substitute holidays that are meaningful to you and your traditions.

• **Prepare**	Easter/spring Preparing for a new beginning
• **Get into State**	Fourth of July Celebrating the independence of the United States.

Remember the Quantum Reading Process by associating it with major holidays.

Prepare
Easter/spring

Get into State
Fourth of July

Use Eye/Hand Skills
Halloween

SuperScan
Thanksgiving

Read
Christmas

Review
New Year's Eve

• Use Eye/Hand Skills	Halloween Mask/costume on eyes/hands.
• SuperScan	Thanksgiving Think of SupperScan, scan- ning all the good food.
• Read	Christmas Santa reading long lists.
• Review	New Year's Eve When you've completed your year (reading), review your year's events.

Remembering Names

In business, remembering names and titles is crucial. The first step to being able to do this is to pay attention when someone tells you his name. If you don't hear it clearly, ask him to repeat it. Then immediately make a connection. The easiest way is to associate the person with someone else you know with the same name.

Before you attend a meeting, if you have a list of who's attending, memorize the name of each person and associate each name with their respective company position. You'll find it's much easier to remember the names when you finally meet these people. Once you're at the meeting, create an immediate association for each person before you hear the name, such as "red sweater," "big earrings," and so on—anything that stands out. (Ideally, I like to find a strong physical feature, but clothing works fine.) Later, you'll associate this person with the item and will remember her name the next time you meet, even though

The ability to remember names and titles is a major benefit in business.

Steps to remembering names:

1 Pay attention when someone tells you his name

2 Repeat the name either to yourself or out loud

3 Immediately make a connection:
- Look for an outstanding physical feature
- Associate with clothing or jewelry
- Connect the name to someone else you know with the same name

she may be wearing something different. An example would be someone in a striped sweater named Sally. You may see the sweater with wavy lines that look like "S's" or imagine the stripes making alleys down the sweater, and that rhymes with Sally.

You can also create associations using outstanding physical features, such as protruding ears, a beard, or long eyelashes. Someone with protruding ears named Frank may make you see franks (sausages) coming out of his ears. Make a game out of it. When you meet someone, notice details immediately and see what kind of association you can create. Memorizing is not only useful, it's fun!

Celebrate Your Learning!

! *Why is having a strong WIIFM especially important to memory?*

It is believed that a part of the brain decides if something is important before it sends it to long-term memory.

! *Which two skills are the basis for memory skills?*

A strong, clear, vivid imagination and the ability to make strong, vivid associations.

! *What elements make information more memorable?*

Being highly aware of your senses and thoroughly experiencing your environment makes things more memorable. Creating exaggerated, outrageous, and absurd images with lots of color, action, and emotion makes them stick in your mind. Also, tie images to your survival and personal importance, use repetition, and create "firsts and lasts."

! *How can you remember names more easily?*

Use association. When you meet someone for the first time, associate an eye-catching article of clothing or physical feature with the person's name. This will make it easier to remember their name the next time you meet.

13

Whatever It Takes: Commitment Makes the Difference

 What are key characteristics of committed people?

 How do you become committed?

 How important is vision to commitment?

 Is commitment always tied to a WIIFM?

On a chilly night in the winter of 1927, a young man stood on the shore of Lake Michigan and stared morosely into the icy water. Thinking himself a total failure, he was about to put an end to his miserable life. Twice he had been expelled from Harvard. He had failed at more jobs than most people hold in their lifetimes. And worst of all, he had lost his infant daughter, Alexandra, to spinal meningitis. His pain was so great, he actually took comfort in the prospect of swimming out into the lake and letting himself drown.

But as he stood there thinking the blackest thoughts, he had a profound revelation. In reviewing his life, he realized that although many of his experiences were negative, they were rich in variety and value. He thought about what an incredible storehouse of experiences each person is, and it occurred to him that he might be able to use some of his experiences to help others avoid the hurt that he had known. He decided to see what would happen if he simply began to look at life differently. He wondered what might result if, instead of focusing on himself, he would commit his life to others.

At that moment the young man committed his life to "making the world work." He began to question and examine nearly every aspect of his life, using what he called "experimental evidence"—discovering things for himself using scientific methods, rather than just accepting them as true.

The young man was R. Buckminster "Bucky" Fuller, and his commitment to "making the world work" resulted in some of the greatest achievements of the twentieth century. Out of Bucky's experimentation came many earth-shaking inventions and ideas. The dymaxion map and the geodesic dome, two of his most famous works, are both

Each person is an incredible storehouse of experiences.

*Buckminster Fuller wondered what might
happen if, instead of focusing on himself,
he would commit his life to others.*

based on his concept of dymaxion: increasing performance using fewer materials—or doing more with less.

During his lifetime, Bucky wrote more than 20 books, held 27 patents, and received 47 honorary doctorate degrees. His work spanned the fields of architecture, design, art, engineering, education, poetry, and mathematics. He has been called the Leonardo da Vinci of our time.

What Bucky discovered that cold, lonely night on the shores of Lake Michigan was commitment. Commitment is doing "Whatever It Takes" to realize your vision. It means throwing yourself full force into a project, jumping in with both feet and immersing yourself in it to a point where you can no longer turn back. Committed people are completely enveloped in their work; it is their passion, their reason for being. They're intrinsically motivated, driven by their dream, propelled by their desire.

Actually, life-changing revelations the magnitude of Bucky's are rare. Most often we hear a quiet, subtle call to commitment. It may not even be a commitment to following our own dream, but to supporting others in furthering their vision.

One such man, Peter Meisen, committed himself to turning Bucky's idea of a global energy network into reality. Bucky developed a plan wherein each of us would share our energy with others during our nonpeak hours at night, thereby ensuring there would be enough energy to supply every country with all their needs. Peter started his quest with only himself and very little capital. But a strong commitment is contagious—a magnetic force, pulling others in, gathering momentum and support. That's just what happened with Peter's project.

"The enormity of the project scared me to death," Peter

recalls, "because it was too big; obviously beyond any one individual. But I had developed enough confidence in a previous project to approach it—not a lot of experience, but a commitment that this could be done if we just started from what we had."

"The first steps were to educate myself personally to understand the technology. I went to the library and I went to the experts themselves. I went to both Mexico and France to meet with engineers."

In 1986 Peter founded the Global Energy Network International (GENI), a nonprofit organization dedicated to realizing Bucky's plan. It took five years to get to GENI's first primary milestone, which was an international workshop in Winnipeg, Alberta, Canada.

Today the power grid concept has been implemented in countries around the world: across the United States; the Nordal system connecting Scandinavia to the rest of Europe; the British Channel link between France and England; and in the former USSR, across seven time zones (over 10,000 kilometers).

While it's difficult to give full credit to Peter for all of this, the fact is many more countries are now linking power systems, and interconnections are accelerating around the world. Since 1989, many former enemies have laid down their weapons and initiated electrical energy sharing in rapid succession. It took East and West Germany just two months to interconnect after the fall of the Berlin Wall, and the Washington Declaration between Jordan and Israel added the linkage of power grids as a prime provision in their peace accords.

GENI's mission statement includes the "commitment to improve the quality of life for all without damage to the planet." Millions of people are now aware of this project through the efforts of Peter and the GENI organization, and Peter continues to win supporters from around the world. His story demonstrates the enormous power contained in the commitment of just one person.

Commit Yourself—And See What Happens

Becoming committed to something is really a two-step process: First you must discover your passion and then you must decide to follow it, no matter what.

Discovery: Think About What Excites You

What turns you on? What fires your passion? What prompts you to dream? What awakens your vision? Before creating the Burklyn Business School and SuperCamp, I had clear pictures in my mind of the possibilities these programs held. I could see, taste, hear, and feel those possibilities, and I felt driven to make them happen.

My partners and I were so excited by the idea of SuperCamp that it carried us through all the uncertainties, problems, and crises of the first program. This excitement was infectious, spreading to others who became eager to send their children on this adventure in learning. At the end of the first SuperCamp, I saw children who had arrived shy and withdrawn stand before the entire group and loudly declare their pride in themselves. They told of their commitment to use their new skills and to live by the 8 Keys.

When I heard them, I was hooked. At that moment I thought, "This is what I am committed to; this is what my life is about—producing programs that support youth." That was 1982 and I am as committed to my vision today as I was on the final day of the first SuperCamp.

Our commitment may be to support the vision of another.

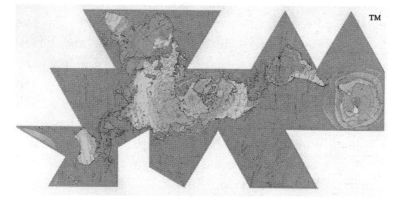

TM

The Dymaxion Map gives a more accurate picture of our world. Dymaxion and the Fuller Projection Dymaxion™ Map design are trademarks of the The Buckminster Fuller Institute, Santa Barbara, CA © 1938, 1967, and 1992. All rights reserved.

Buckminster Fuller's concept of a power grid is being implemented around the world, thanks in part to Peter Meisen's commitment to his vision.

Decision

Once you discover what your vision is, you must decide whether you're willing to do Whatever It Takes to make that vision real. How much time, money, and energy are you willing to put forth? What sort of impact will this have on your family, friends, and finances? Are you ready to throw yourself into this project whole-heartedly and without regret? Is this the right time in your life to make this commitment?

When you have a powerful vision, it may seem as if you have no choice but to commit. You have to see the project through. Your goal is clear and compelling and you're driven to make it real, despite the obstacles you may face.

Every new business starts with one person being committed to making a vision come true. This one person must have the tenacity to continue until he or she reaches the goal. When I started the first SuperCamp program, I could visualize it, I could see where it would be ten years down the line. Bucky said, "Find something that needs to be done, and do it." SuperCamp was certainly something that needed doing, and I was excited and driven to do it.

When I first made the commitment to start SuperCamp, I had a clear picture of what the program would be like—but that was about all I had. This was shortly after I had lost all my money in stock options, so my resources were extremely limited. But it didn't matter what it would take to put the program on; I knew we could do it.

Taking a loan against my car, the only asset I had left, I financed the first program. It didn't feel like a sacrifice or hardship because there was no question in my mind about doing it or not doing it. I was eager and committed to making it happen.

Commitment is driven by your WIIFM, and it's usually

Commitment is crossing the line to being willing to do Whatever It Takes.

Until one is committed, there is hesitancy, the chance to draw back, always ineffectiveness. Concerning all acts of initiative (and creation), there is one elementary truth, the ignorance of which kills countless ideas and splendid plans: the moment one definitely commits oneself, then Providence moves too. All sorts of things occur to help one that would never otherwise have occurred. A whole stream of events issues from the decision, raising in one's favor all manner of unforeseen incidents and meetings and material assistance, which no man could have dreamt would have come his way. I have learned a deep respect for one of Goethe's couplets:

Whatever you can do,
or dream you can, begin it.
Boldness has genius, power,
and magic in it.

William Hutchinson Murray
The Scottish Himalayan Expedition 1950
(J.M. Dent, London, 1951)

something bigger than financial gain. It might simply be the joy and satisfaction of seeing your vision come to realization.

At SuperCamp, my commitment was affirmed after the first program, when I saw the students stand up and express themselves so eloquently. My WIIFM continues to be the inspiring letters and calls I get from my SuperCamp graduates and their parents. After hearing of their accomplishments I can't help but think, "Yes, this is why I'm committed to doing what I do. This is why I'm willing to do Whatever It Takes to continue my vision."

Commitment can be tied to a principle, to satisfaction in the happiness of others, and to profits for yourself. Back when I was at Hawthorne/Stone, one of our major projects was a condominium conversion of an apartment complex with 540 tenants, many of them retired. You can imagine how the tenants felt when we first visited the site after purchasing the property. I distinctly remember walking across the grounds while people stared at us skeptically from their windows. They were suspicious of us and worried about what would become of them and their homes.

But we were committed to making the conversion a "win" for everyone, so we started by talking privately with the tenants, getting to know them, and learning their dreams and desires. We talked publicly about our plans and even held open forums where we encouraged the tenants to ask questions. At the beginning of the process most of the tenants didn't even know each other and rarely smiled or spoke. By the end, we had happy, smiling tenants actually campaigning on our behalf. On their own initiative, they took city council members to lunch, telling them why they—the tenants—wanted the conversion. The council had never before approved a conversion and was reluctant to do so. If they had encountered any opposition from the tenants, they would have eagerly used it as an excuse to reject our proposal.

By listening to our tenants, we learned much about their desires, needs, and challenges. Many of them had dreamed for years of owning their own homes, yet felt they had no hope of making that dream a reality. Using various creative means, we were able to offer them the apartment/condos at special, affordable rates and terms. We also made arrangements for long-time tenants to continue to rent at reasonable rates. On the day of the hearing, the council chamber was standing room only with people spilling into the hallways. A steady stream of tenants testified on our behalf, and the conversion was approved.

I believe this happened because of our commitment to making it a win/win situation for everyone involved—the investors, the bank, our tenants, and ourselves. Many times we faced obstacles we thought were insurmountable. And we overcame them. Every new challenge was an opportunity to do Whatever It Took to accomplish our goal. We listened to the tenants' desires and structured the conversion to fill their needs as well as ours. We turned many tenants into happy homeowners, and made millions of dollars in the process. The WIIFM was making people happy and improving their situation while making money for ourselves and our clients.

Are You a Thermometer or a Thermostat?

When it comes to commitment and living your life, you can choose to be either a thermometer or a thermostat. A thermometer is just a little glass tube with a small quantity of mercury inside. Put it in a refrigerator and the mercury will shrink; move it into the sunshine and the mercury will expand. The thermometer achieves nothing; it changes nothing. It simply reflects its surroundings. Choose to be a thermometer and you're choosing to remain comfortable, having no impact on the world, avoiding challenges and change.

By contrast, a thermostat has the power to change its surroundings. Move the switch on a thermostat and it can make the temperature in a room go from winter to summer. Commitment to a clear vision gives you the power to effect change. Rather than adapt to your "lot in life" and reflect your surroundings like a thermometer, you have the potential, like a thermostat, to change them. You can remake your circumstances to reflect your vision. As you recognize and learn to use the power of commitment, you can make your life an exciting, fulfilling challenge.

Like Bucky Fuller, like Peter Meisen, and like everyone who's ever succeeded at something difficult, simply by being willing to do Whatever It Takes, you can literally change the world.

Celebrate Your Learning!

 What are key characteristics of committed people?

Committed people are intrinsically motivated and driven by their dreams.

 How do you become committed?

Commitment is a two-step process:

1. Discover your passion.
2. Decide to follow it, no matter what.

 How important is vision to commitment?

Very important. When you have a powerful vision, it may seem as if you have no choice but to commit.

 Is commitment always tied to a WIIFM?

Commitment can also be tied to a principle, or to satisfaction in the happiness of others.

14

More Memory Magic with Peg Systems

 What are the advantages to learning a memory system, like a peg list?

 How can you memorize the Phonetic Peg List?

 How can you use pegs to memorize a long number, like a telephone number?

 What other kinds of things can be memorized with pegs?

Y ou've already discovered the incredible power of your memory. You learned how to use imagination, association, linking, and location to memorize lists, people's names, the 8 Keys, or anything else you need stored in your brain. Now you're ready to master a more advanced and extremely powerful memory system: the Phonetic Peg System.

Peg Systems

Peg systems are a way of remembering things by associating them with a basic list of numbers and items. A basic system usually consists of 15 to 20 numbers. You start by creating a list—associating an item with each number. For example, "sun" might be number one, "shoe" number two, and so on. For easier memorization, it helps to choose an item that rhymes, such as "one" "sun" and "two" "shoe" or using something that relates to the number, such as "two" and "eyes." For the peg system to be useful, the words and their order must be so well known that they become second nature to you—you don't even have to think about them. This takes some work, but once you learn the list, you're able to memorize all sorts of information, just by associating it with your pegs.

The Phonetic Peg System

The Phonetic Peg System is the most powerful of all the peg systems. You can use it for simple associations as well as for complex lists and numbers. It can help you remember where you parked your car at the county fair and that list of 20 client telephone numbers you call frequently. Practice will make it easier to use. But be forewarned, you must commit to memorizing the system before you can use it—and that might take you a while. I spent a week learning the numbers and attached items, practicing

Peg systems associate what you want to remember with a basic list of numbers and items.

To be useful,

the items and their

associated numbers

must be so well known

they become

second-nature to you.

them as I drove around town. You can practice anywhere—waiting in the doctor's office, standing by the carousel waiting for your luggage to arrive, or just lying in bed at night. When I began learning the Phonetic Peg System, throughout the day and night, I recited the peg words for numbers I saw. If I woke during the night, I would glance at my digital clock and mentally say the peg words for the numbers on the clock!

The Phonetic Peg System uses a list of numbers from 0 to 100. (My own version of it includes 00 through 09, which can be quite useful, as you'll see later.) Each number has an item associated with it. The numbers and items together provide a base to which you then attach or associate what you're trying to remember. You literally hang the information on the pegs.

Tony Buzan writes in *Use Your Perfect Memory* (Penguin Group, New York, 1991), the Phonetic Peg System was developed in the 17th century by Stanislaus Mink von Wennsshein, and modified in the 18th century by Dr. Richard Grey. It was developed for memorizing lists of any length, order, or structure and was highly valued at a time when memorizing stories and information was critical because copying, all of which was done by hand, was costly and time-consuming.

Learning the System

The Phonetic Peg System is great for remembering series of numbers (phone numbers, business statistics, etc.), and to use as a general peg system for anything you want to remember. To learn the system, first memorize the consonant or phonetic sounds associated with the numbers 0–9.

Use the Phonetic Peg System for simple associations or more complex lists and numbers.

Commit time and energy to mastering this method:

1 Memorize the phonetic sounds associated with the numbers 0–9

2 Memorize the word for 0, 10, 20, 30, 40, 50, 60, 70 . . . This will be your anchor for the next step

3 Memorize the numbers and words in each group of ten, i.e., 0–9, 10–19, 20–29, 30–39 . . .

The Phonetic Alphabet

This is both an auditory and visual system, so it's difficult to explain it strictly with words on a page. But I've modified the system to make it easier to learn. You can remember the numbers 0-9 and their attached sounds by using the following associations:

Number	Phonetic Sound	Mental Triggers
0 =	sa, za ca (soft c)	S0S – S(Zer0)S
1 =	ma	M1 – M1 rifle
2 =	ra	R2 – R2D2 from "Star Wars"
3 =	da, ta	3D – 3 Dimensional 3D glasses
4 =	na	4N – Foreign
5 =	ja, sha, cha ga (soft g), dg, tch	J5 – Jackson 5, shortened to Ja5 singing "Chattanooga Choo Choo"
6 =	pa, ba	6P – 6 pack
7 =	la	7L – 7-Eleven convenience store
8 =	va, fa, pha ga (hard g)	V8 – V-8 juice, Fay Vincent drinking V-8 in a Fiat
9 =	ka, ca (hard c)	K9 – Canine, Go, canine

Notice you use the same mouth shape to say the sounds for each number.

Here are mental triggers to help you remember the phonetic alphabet.

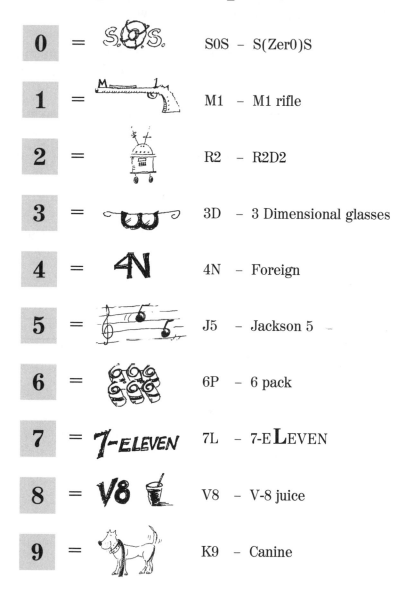

0	=	S O S	SOS – S(Zer0)S
1	=	M1 rifle	M1 – M1 rifle
2	=	R2	R2 – R2D2
3	=	3D	3D – 3 Dimensional glasses
4	=	4N	4N – Foreign
5	=	J5	J5 – Jackson 5
6	=	6P	6P – 6 pack
7	=	7-ELEVEN	7L – 7-ELEVEN
8	=	V8	V8 – V-8 juice
9	=	K9	K9 – Canine

The Peg List

To create a peg list, you can come up with words that have the phonetic sounds of the numbers from 0 to 100. Or you can simply memorize the peg list on the right-hand page that my son Grant and I developed. Vowels and the letters H, Q, Y, W, X aren't associated with any number and are used only to complete words, as in HOME, which is a word that conveys the "mmmm" sound. Since 1=M, and the bare "mmmm" sound is not a word, I used the letters H, O, and E to create a word that represents the number 1.

As another example, let's look at the first word on the list. For the number zero, the associated sound is s or z. We add vowels and an "H" to create the peg word—in this case "hose." Since the letter H and the vowels O and E don't represent a number, we're left with "S," which is zero. To simplify the memorizing, the list is broken down by tens and the ten words in each group mostly start with the same consonant.

How to Memorize the Peg List

To start memorizing the pegs, create pictures in your mind of the 10 words. This will help you remember a specific series and you can start at any point on the list; you needn't start with one.

For 10, (1=M, 0=S), see a prize moose wearing a big blue ribbon with a number 10 around its neck.

For 20, (2=R, 0=S), see 20 prize rose bushes (a little less than 2 dozen) in the garden. They cost me $20 each!

For 30, (3=D, 0=S/soft C), picture dice with little 30's printed all over them.

For 40, see a nose with a long, narrow 40 tattooed on it.

For 50, think of the "Juice Man," a man who's 50 years old and in great shape from drinking juice.

The Phonetic Peg List:

0 Hose	10 Moose	20 Rose	30 Dice	40 Nose	50 Juice
1 Home	11 Mom	21 Ram	31 Dam	41 Name	51 Jam
2 Hair	12 Mare	22 Rear	32 Deer	42 Narrow	52 Jar
3 Hat	13 Mitt	23 Road	33 Dad	43 Net	53 Jet
4 Hen	14 Moon	24 Rain	34 Den	44 Nun	54 Chain
5 Hash	15 Mush	25 Rush	35 Dish	45 Nudge	55 Judge
6 Hobo	16 Map	26 Rope	36 Dip(stick)	46 Nap	56 Ship
7 Hill	17 Mail	27 Rail	37 Dial	47 Nail	57 Shell
8 Hive	18 Movie	28 Reef	38 Dove	48 Navy	58 Chef
9 Hook	19 Mic(rophone)	29 Rake	39 Duck	49 Neck	59 Check

60 Bus	70 Lace	80 Face	90 Case	100 Moses	00 Sauce
61 Beam	71 Lamb	81 Foam	91 Comb		01 Sum
62 Bear	72 Lure	82 Fire	92 Car		02 Soar
63 Bat	73 Light	83 Feet	93 Cat		03 Seat
64 Bone	74 Lion	84 Fan	94 Can		04 Sun
65 Beach	75 Leash	85 Fish	95 Cash		05 Sash
66 Baby	76 Lab	86 Fib	96 Cab		06 Sap
67 Ball	77 Lily	87 File	97 Coal		07 Sail
68 Beef	78 Leaf	88 Fife	98 Cave		08 Safe
69 Bike	79 Lake	89 Fig	99 Cake		09 Sock

For 60, see a 60's type hippie bus.

For 70, see lace with a 70 crocheted in the middle.

For 80, see the face of an 80-year-old woman.

For 90, see a sunglasses case with the designer name 'ninety' imprinted on it

Linking the Pegs
The most difficult part of this system is to initially memorize this list. For me, it helps to link the pegs in a story.

0-9
Start with <u>hose</u> (0). See a hose laid out in the shape of a big circle (like a 0) on your front lawn. See the door of your <u>home</u> shaped like a large #1. Inside is a person with long <u>hair</u>. See her 2 braids sticking up and shaped like R's. See a <u>hat</u> on her head shaped with 3 points sticking up. Then see a very strange <u>hen</u> with 4 legs pulling off the hat and then falling into a plate of <u>hash</u> on the table and walking across it. See the imprint of the hen's 5 toes in the hash. See a <u>hobo</u> (6) sitting on a chair at the table hungrily looking at the hash. The hobo then gets up, as he doesn't like it, and goes outside to walk up a <u>hill</u> (7) where he sees a <u>hive</u> (8) hanging from a <u>hook</u> (9).

Tens
See the <u>moose</u> with the blue ribbon with the 10 around his neck. See <u>Mom</u> standing next to the moose, petting it with her hand. Her other hand is petting a <u>mare</u> that is 12 hands high. This mare is strange . . . it has a <u>mitt</u> on its foot and it looks especially eerie with the <u>moon</u>light shining down on it. The mare walks forward and steps into <u>mush</u> that's lying on top of a <u>map</u>, which shows him which direction to go to <u>mail</u> a letter before seeing a <u>movie</u> where every seat is equipped with a <u>mic</u>rophone.

A powerful memory requires the ability to visualize what you're trying to remember.

Here's a visual picture for remembering the pegs for 0-9.

0 = Hose
1 = Home
2 = Hair
3 = Hat
4 = Hen
5 = Hash
6 = Hobo
7 = Hill
8 = Hive
9 = Hook

Twenties

See 20 prize <u>rose</u>bushes in a garden. A <u>ram</u> charges out of the garden and into the <u>rear</u> of a car that's on a <u>road</u>. Then the <u>rain</u> comes down and the car <u>rush</u>es away. Someone ties a <u>rope</u> to the car to slow it down but it runs onto a <u>rail</u>, which it follows, then it falls into a <u>reef</u> where someone is raking the bottom with a <u>rake</u>.

Thirties

See <u>dice</u> with 30's printed all over them. Throw the dice and see them falling over a <u>dam</u>. At the edge of the water below the dam is a <u>deer</u>, and <u>Dad</u> comes out of the woods to look at the deer. He goes home to sit in his <u>den</u> and eats ice cream off a <u>dish</u> with a <u>dip</u>stick. He then <u>dials</u> his phone and says to the person on the other end, "My goodness, a <u>dove</u> just flew past the window and now a <u>duck</u> is walking by."

Forties

See a <u>nose</u> with a narrow 40 written down it. It's the <u>name</u> of the nose and it's written very <u>narrow</u> because it's a narrow nose. And over the head (and the nose) is a <u>net</u>. It's a <u>nun</u>'s nose and net, and she gives a <u>nudge</u> to someone who's taking a <u>nap</u> on a bed of <u>nails</u>. This someone is in the <u>Navy</u>. I know because he's wearing a uniform. On his <u>neck</u> I notice a tattoo that reads '49.'

Fifties

Think of the "<u>Juice</u> Man," 50 years old and still in great shape from drinking juice. See him sitting at the breakfast table eating <u>jam</u> and juice out of a <u>jar</u>. He runs out the door to catch a <u>jet</u> plane that can't take off as it's held down by <u>chains</u>. A <u>judge</u> confirms it: "You can't take off." So he leaves by <u>ship</u> and takes a <u>shell</u> from the beach to give to the <u>chef</u> who wrote him a <u>check</u> for his food.

Here's a visual picture for remembering the pegs for 30-39.

30 = Dice
31 = Dam
32 = Deer
33 = Dad
34 = Den
35 = Dish
36 = Dip(stick)
37 = Dial
38 = Dove
39 = Duck

Sixties

See a 60's hippie <u>bus</u>. Light <u>beam</u>s are shooting out of the bus. Through the beams you see a <u>bear</u> who runs into a baseball <u>bat</u>, which makes him dizzy. He has a <u>bone</u> in his mouth and he's running and running to the <u>beach</u> where there's a <u>baby</u> playing with a <u>ball</u>. The ball flies up and lands on the <u>beef</u> on a barbecue that has a <u>bike</u> leaning against it.

Seventies

See a beautiful, dainty piece of <u>lace</u> with the number 70 crocheted in the middle of it. This lace is now around the neck of a <u>lamb</u> and pinned together with a fishing <u>lure</u>. The lamb is standing in the bright sun<u>light</u> and is spotted by a <u>lion</u> who runs after it. The lion has a <u>leash</u> around its neck, which trails behind as the big cat runs. It runs right up to a <u>lab</u> building with a <u>lily</u> by the front door, which has a beautiful <u>leaf</u>. The whole scene reflects on the nearby <u>lake</u>.

Eighties

See the wrinkled <u>face</u> of an 80-year-old woman. In her hand is an extinguisher shooting <u>foam</u> at a <u>fire</u>. Her <u>feet</u> are hot and she's jumping up and down. To cool her feet she holds them up in front of a <u>fan</u>. The fan blows a <u>fish</u> smell that's very unpleasant. A man nearby <u>fib</u>s and says, "There is no fish!" And you can see there is a fish in a <u>file</u> folder. To distract you, he plays a <u>fife</u> and offers you a fake <u>fig</u> to eat.

Nineties

See an eyeglasses <u>case</u> with the designer brand "90" imprinted on it. Inside is a <u>comb</u> rather than glasses and the case is sitting on the hood of a <u>car</u>. A <u>cat</u> that's also on the hood wakes up and jumps off the car, landing on a <u>can</u> that turns over and spills out <u>cash</u>. Take the cash and jump

And here's a picture for 60-69:

60	=	Bus
61	=	Beam
62	=	Bear
63	=	Bat
64	=	Bone
65	=	Beach
66	=	Baby
67	=	Ball
68	=	Beef
69	=	Bike

in a <u>cab</u> and drive over some <u>coal</u> and into a <u>cave</u>. Inside there's light from the glow of candles on a birthday <u>cake</u>.

00-09

I found it helpful to also have associations for the numbers 00-09, as many phone numbers and other important numbers are made up of these figures. For these numbers you can: see a large pot of <u>sauce</u> that includes the <u>sum</u> of all the ingredients. And as you complete adding the ingredients, you see a glider plane <u>soar</u>ing overhead so you take a <u>seat</u> in the <u>sun</u> to watch. You wear a <u>sash</u> across yourself to protect you from the sun and also from the <u>sap</u> that falls from a tree. It's not enough protection, so you cover yourself with a <u>sail</u> and you feel <u>safe</u>. Especially as you also put on a <u>sock</u>.

If you forget a word, you have only to think of the phonetic sound the number represents and usually the word will come to you. If it doesn't, go back to the previous ten (that is, 10, 20, 30, etc.) and repeat the story to yourself. In a second it should come to you. If you still can't think of the word, make up another word that fits with the sound.

Whenever possible, a peg word should be a noun, something you can actually see. Notice above, I said, 'You see a glider plane soaring overhead.' The word is <u>soar</u>, so I added a glider plane (noun)—something you can see. Also, instead of *taking* a seat, *see* a seat (chair/bench). Instead of *feeling* safe, *see* a safe (vault). Instead of a vague sum, see a list of ingredients with plus signs beside them.

Examples of Ways to Use the Phonetic Peg System

You'll find unlimited uses for this peg system. Use it to remember numbers, speeches, facts, "to-do" lists, directions, just about anything you want to remember.

For example, I use it to remember how much weight to use on each piece of workout equipment at the gym. I found it awkward carrying around a sheet of paper so I could look up the weight at each station. I solved that problem. Here's how I remember:

• Leg press:	70	Loose	(different from lace but works, L = 7 and S = 0) I start by imagining my legs getting loose.
• Leg Extensions:	25	Rush	I then rush to the next leg machines.
• Leg Curls:			(same image as leg extensions)
• Chest Press:	20	Rose	I picture a long-stemmed red rose lying across my chest, and know that rose is related to all the upper body machines.
• Shoulder press:	15	Mush	For the shoulder press I have to pump my arms up and down. This is one machine where I picture myself making mush out of the rose.

• Lat Pulls:	20	Rose
• Seated Row:	20	Rose
• Hip:	40	I kNowS ($N = 4$, $S = 0$) H.A.T. (hip, ab, thigh) is 40
• Abdominal:	40	
• Thigh:	40	
• Glute (buttock):	20	but the butt with the tattooed rose is 20.

These associations are silly and not grammatically correct, but they work. Remember, crazy sights help our recall.

Learning Computer Software

You can also use the Phonetic Peg System to memorize computer commands. In our software program, Paradox, F1 is Help and our peg for 1 is home. Think of coming <u>home</u> for help. F2 is "Do It" and our peg for 2 is hair. Picture a fancy <u>hair</u> "do." F7 is toggle and our 7 is hill. Think of a <u>hill</u> with a giant toggle on top of it, throwing you from one side to the other. F9 is edit and our 9 is hook. See a tiny <u>hook</u> going over each line, hooking letters and pulling them out of the words. Come up with your own methods for your computer programs.

Learning Numbers

A great application of the Phonetic Peg System is to use it for remembering phone numbers. For example, take the

There are many ways to make use of your Phonetic Peg System.

You can even use it to remember how much weight to use on workout equipment!

phone number (320) 478-0082. (By the way, this is no one's number, so don't bother to dial it.)

1. First, associate the numbers with our phonetic words. See 3 = hat, 20 = rose. Picture the person whose number this is, say her name is Jill, wearing a hat decorated with roses.

2. Next, see 4 = hen, 78 = leaf, 00 = sauce, 82 = fire. Then picture a hen running after Jill, so it can eat a rose . . . but really it's the leaf that the hen is after. Jill starts to run and steps into a pot of sauce left cooking over an open fire.

This is nonsensical, but if your images are strong and vivid, it will stay with you. I chose random numbers to illustrate how images that are not logically connected can be linked together.

I've taken groups of phone numbers I want to remember, such as those of our 20 staff members at the office, and written words for each of their numbers. This makes it easier for me to first make the connections and then to review them. I've also listed other personal numbers that I want to remember such as my passport and driver's license numbers, and memorized them all at one time. I write these on an index card that I carry around so that I can easily review the numbers whenever I have a moment, like when waiting in lines.

Memorizing Quantum Business

Here is an example to remember key elements to successful working environments by using our Phonetic Peg System. This time I used the thirties.

The Phonetic Peg System is great for remembering all kinds of numbers.

To remember a phone number, or any long number, break it down into groups of one or two numbers, and attach the peg word.

(320) 478-0082

(3   20)   4   78 - 00   82
 hat   rose   hen   leaf   sauce   fire

30 **Dice** Clear Vision
See yourself walking and wearing an
unusual pair of glasses. The lenses are
actually a large clear pair of dice, and they
provide excellent vision.

31 **Dam** Mission Statement
Picture a Spanish mission sitting near a
dam. The water splashes up on you as you
sit outside the mission.

32 **Deer** Alignment on Principles and Beliefs
See deer standing in alignment, one after
the other. They are highly principled and
you can't believe what your eyes are seeing.

33 **Dad** High level of Safety and Trust
Your dad provides a high level of safety
and trust.

34 **Den** Strong Relationships
Strong relationships are created when
friends gather in the den.

35 **Dish** Visible Communication
See a huge satellite dish delivering very
visible communication to your TV.

Now practice applying the memory skills to your own
life. There are many ways to remember any list, be it a "to-
do" list, a list of key points in a speech, a book, a system or
a list of words. Pick the method that is easiest for you to
remember.

Use memory techniques to recall information presented in this book.

Remember the key elements in creating successful work environments:

Clear vision

::

Mission statement

::

Alignment on principles and beliefs

::

Safety and trust

::

Strong relationships

::

Visible communication

Experiment with association, location, linking, and pegs. Discover for yourself the value of a powerful memory. You may want to use different systems for different situations, such as location for speeches, association for names, a combination of phonetic pegs, and linking for numbers.

It takes an extra effort at first, but keep practicing until the systems become natural for you. Be committed for one week and practice throughout each day. Before long, both you and your associates will be amazed at the power of your memory.

Celebrate Your Learning!

! *What are the advantages to learning a memory system, like a peg list?*

A memory system enables you to remember massive amounts of information with very little effort. And, there's no need to waste time looking up frequently used information. It saves time, reduces stress, and supports your success.

! *How can you memorize the Phonetic Peg List?*

First, learn the phonetic alphabet. Then, break the list into sets of 10 and create pictures in your mind of the peg items. Link the pegs in an imaginative story. The more outrageous the story, the easier it is to remember. If you forget an item, make the sounds the number represents. It should pop into your mind.

! *How can you use pegs to memorize a long number, like a telephone number?*

Break the long number down into several small numbers and attach peg words to these numbers.

! *What other kinds of things can be memorized with pegs?*

The Phonetic Peg System can be used to memorize nearly anything. Use it for speeches, computer commands, sales figures, employee names, or Quantum Business techniques.

15

This Is It!

 Why should you have a "This Is It" attitude?

 What benefits can you expect by focusing on the task at hand?

 What kinds of things distract you from focusing on the present?

 How do you make "This Is It" out of things you don't enjoy?

I have a friend who's always waiting for something to happen in the future. He believes that then he'll live his life fully. At work every day, he watches the clock, counting the minutes until quitting time. He can't wait to get home to relax and enjoy himself. He thinks that when he gets home, that will be IT. At home, though, chores and various personal responsibilities overwhelm him, and he hopes the weekdays will pass quickly so he can enjoy the weekend. He's convinced the weekend will be IT. But the weekend is disappointing. Coming and going in a flash, it rarely lives up to his expectations. Next weekend, he thinks, things will be different. Next weekend will be IT. Meanwhile, Monday comes and the cycle begins all over again.

Possibly you have a friend like this, or you may recognize this trait in yourself. As you're waiting for the next moment to arrive, the present—which is really the only time you ever have—slips away.

Whenever your mind is occupied with something other than what you're doing, you miss the opportunity for a valuable experience. If you worry about work while you attend your son's Little League game, you can miss his first home run, or fail to understand why he's so upset about losing. You're really not there. If you choose to stay at work and miss the game, you may spend your work hours feeling guilty about not spending time with your son. It's not uncommon to feel torn between work and family, but by always making something else IT, you lose what's going on around you in the moment. It could happen occasionally, and you may lose a few moments. Or it could happen constantly and you may be missing your whole life.

Some people are experts at making their life IT. A marvelous example of this is a young woman from the

Live in the present — make today IT.

By making something else IT, you miss what's going on around you in the moment.

Midwest whom I greatly admire. In 1983, she was ranked third-best high diver in her state, only 2.5 points behind the first-place diver. Today she's preparing herself to become a world champion high diver. Recently she was given an award for typing 43 words per minute. Most typists know that 43 words per minute is no great accomplishment. But for this woman it is—because she has no arms! Despite a serious handicap, she sees herself as a winner and believes in herself. She sees life as an adventure and makes the most of every moment, stretching her abilities and beliefs about what she can achieve. Rather than letting her handicap limit her, she looks at her situation as a whole and says, "This Is It." She then goes on to beat overwhelming odds and accomplish great things.

Turning Now into "It"

Think of what will happen if you make the most of every moment and always focus on the task at hand. You'll do better work, enjoy what you're doing more, and get more out of it. By putting all your energy into your current projects, you'll begin to see them differently. You'll find shortcuts for routine tasks and solutions to old problems. You may even develop greater insight and intuition about your work. Life is more exciting when you live it now instead of waiting for the future to arrive.

So what's holding you back? Does a little voice in your head distract you from the present? Some people are unaware of the voices in their heads. Right now you may be saying to yourself, "What voice? I don't hear a voice, I don't talk to myself, that's absurd!" Listen carefully ... that's the voice. While you relax in your favorite chair, it's whispering to you about chores that need to be done or unfinished projects that need your attention. It fills your present moments with thoughts of things you should have done differently, or what you're going to do next. It shifts your focus away from the present.

The voice in your head may do more than take your focus off the present moment, it may also eat away at your self-confidence. You may hear the voice telling you: "You don't know how to do this. You're not smart enough." Or: "If you do that, people will think you're crazy!"

That little voice is powerful; it can influence whether you succeed or fail. Successful people have learned that if the inner voice says you'll fail, you will. If it says you'll succeed, you will. In the words of comedian Whoopi Goldberg: "The only cuss words I know are 'I can't.'"

If you're going to live fully, if you're going to make every moment "it," you need to take control of the voice in your head and use it to your advantage. First, become aware of what you're telling yourself. Tune in to those comments in your head. Are they supportive and uplifting, or negative and debilitating? Whenever you hear the voice begin a negative statement, make a conscious choice to shift the tone to a positive one. "I can do this." "I'm an intelligent person, fully capable of understanding how to do this." Stay in the present moment. If you find yourself dreaming about the future or past, tell yourself "I live in the present moment. I focus my attention on what I'm doing now!"

The Value of Reframing

You may be thinking "It's fine to focus on things I enjoy. But what about doing things I hate? Shouldn't I try to think about something else to make the work more enjoyable?" The answer is no, you should "reframe,"—change the way you look at the task, rather than doing the task while looking the other way. What you perceive is reality for you.

Let me say that again. What you perceive—what you see from your point of view—that's reality, that's what's real for you. If you don't like the reality you've created around doing certain things, change that reality for a better one. You change the reality simply by changing the way you look at it—whether the external circumstances are altered or not.

"Reframing" is taking a negative picture we hold in our minds and looking at it from a new angle, or framing it differently. Think back to Chapter 4, when you learned about the power of WIIFM. When you're faced with an unpleasant task or situation and need to make the most of it, discover value in it. It may not be the task itself that's so important, but rather the character you build by following through and doing your best. Whatever it is, you'll get more value out of it once you use "This Is It."

Creating This Is It in Your Business

Make the most of every moment and opportunity in your business by keeping the big picture in mind. Take a look at where your company/career is. What do you need to do to move forward? Be upfront about things that need to change. Create This Is It by learning from the situation and looking for solutions.

You can use This Is It to encourage cooperation and teamwork. At Learning Forum, we sometimes have large projects like stuffing thousands of envelopes or packing materials in preparation for a camp or seminar, and the mailing houses can't always meet our deadlines. When these minor emergencies crop up, we use This Is It to turn the monster project into a group activity.

Everyone knows the task is important. In the big picture, it means reaching our clients, which in turn means making

Make the most of
every moment.

*If you make the
most of
every moment,
you'll do
better work,
enjoy what
you're doing,
and get more
out of it.*

sales and staying in business. When everyone pitches in, the task gets done quickly, we spend time together, and we have fun.

You can also create This Is It for the tasks you can't share. Look over your "to-do" list in the morning, star the things you don't want to do or have been putting off, and do them first. Get them out of the way early so they won't be hanging over your head the rest of the day. You'll feel a sense of accomplishment and relief and will be free to concentrate on other matters.

Sometimes This Is It can help us face a crisis. In 1991, the combination of the Gulf War and the U.S. economic slump caused a sudden decrease in SuperCamp enrollments, hitting us hard financially. We had to make some difficult decisions about cutbacks and layoffs, but we didn't abandon our basic principle of open communication. We held a meeting with the staff and were honest with them about our financial situation and the impact it would have on them. It was one of the most difficult meetings I've ever had to conduct. I wanted to avoid it, but I had to make it This Is It and be honest with everyone.

I was amazed by the level of trust and support I received from the staff. Everyone started brainstorming ideas on how we could get through this period. Some people offered to defer their paychecks for three months, and one man even offered to lend us his personal savings. The staff trusted us and strongly believed in the value of our programs. Using This Is It, they pulled together to make the most of their resources and keep the company going.

If you can make the most of every moment, you're well on your way to becoming more productive and living a more fulfilling life. Keep in tune with the present moment, and make it count. You only have one life and . . . This Is It!

Celebrate Your Learning!

! *Why should you have a "This Is IT" attitude?*

Whenever your mind is occupied with something other than what you're doing, you miss the opportunity for a valuable experience.

! *What benefits can you expect by focusing on the task at hand?*

You'll do better at work, and enjoy what you're doing more. You'll also find shortcuts for projects and develop greater insight into your work.

! *What kinds of things distract you from focusing on the present?*

The voice in your head that says things like "You don't know how to do this!" If you're going to live fully, you need to take control of the voice in your head and use it to your advantage.

! *How do you make "This Is It" out of things you don't enjoy?*

By "reframing" the situation—changing the way you look at a task.

16

Creative Thinking, Planning, and Problem-Solving

 Why is it important to use your creative abilities?

 What is one of the first things you need to bring out creativity in people?

 What traits do creative thinkers have?

 What are the steps to creative planning and problem-solving?

Business owners and employees today face a number of challenges that have never come up before in history. In his book, *101 Creative Problem-Solving Techniques* (New Management, Winter Park, Florida, 1994), James M. Higgins details several of those challenges:

- Businesses are becoming increasingly global.
- Competition is intensifying.
- New technology is being introduced at a phenomenal rate.
- Workforce demographics are changing.
- Critical resources are in short supply.
- The U.S. is transforming from an industrial economy to an economy based on knowledge and information.

Each of these areas of change offers opportunities, but you and your organization need creative thought and foresight to take advantage of them. "To transform an organization you must first transform its thinking," writes Joyce Wycoff in *Transformational Thinking* (Berkley, New York, 1995). You can start preparing for that transformation now by building thinking skills in every member of your organization. Do that, says Wycoff, and here's what you can expect:

"When an organization commits to creating an environment which stimulates the growth of everyone in the organization, amazing things start to happen: ideas pop up everywhere, people start to work together instead of 'playing politics,' new opportunities appear; customers begin to notice service and attitude improvements; collections of individuals begin to coalesce into teams."

Creativity Is a Skill
We're all creative beings, but when we fail to exercise

Turn business changes into business opportunities.

Use creative thought and foresight to take advantage of opportunities.

our creativity regularly, it atrophies like the little-used muscles of a desk jockey. The results of a test given to measure creativity in different age groups illustrates this point. Reported in *Break-Point and Beyond* by George Land (Harper Business, New York, 1992), the test showed five-year-olds scoring 98 percent, ten-year-olds 32 percent, 15-year-olds 10 percent, and adults only 2 percent.

Unlike adults, young children give their creative thinking skills a regular workout. They're always examining and questioning, and their favorite question is "Why?" Sometimes, it seems they believe nothing adults tell them until they've run their own tests and formed their own conclusions. Later, kids learn to follow the rules and accept the information they receive without question.

When you progressed toward adulthood, by learning to limit your behavior you increased your chances for acceptance in society—but you also limited your creativity. Fortunately, you can relearn to exercise your creative skills by challenging yourself to ask questions, reach your own conclusions, and see things from new angles.

Most people associate creativity with artists and inventors, but you don't have to invent a new mousetrap or paint a Mona Lisa to be considered creative. You're involved in creative activity on a smaller scale every day. You do things like plan parties, decorate your home, and create new systems to better organize your office. That's creativity. And these activities make good starting places for building your creative thinking abilities.

The Creative Environment
Creative thinking starts with the right environment, one that includes the creative planning and problem-solving process, and nourishes the creative thinker. To get the

Recapture your childhood curiosity and creativity.

Be involved in creative activity every day:

Challenge yourself to ask questions

::

Reach your own conclusions

::

See things from new angles

most out of the creative minds at your business, you must build an environment that supports creative thought.

As I mentioned in Chapter 2, for everyone to perform their best you must lay a foundation of trust and safety. This is especially true when it comes to creativity. If people fear their ideas will be laughed at, stolen, or simply ignored, they won't speak up and share the brilliant insights that could save your company time or money right now.

Author James M. Higgins defines innovation as the "process of creating something new that has significant value to an individual, a group, an organization, an industry or a society." If the organization's culture doesn't support or require innovation, it's unlikely innovation will occur. Innovation results from careful management of the organizational culture—that is, encouraging people to look for areas that could work better and to use creative thinking to discover solutions. People are innovative when they know they'll be taken seriously. It's vital, therefore, for your organization to make employees feel their contributions are worthy, new ideas will be carefully considered, and creative thinking will not be stifled.

By the Rules

When striving to create an open environment, take a look at your company's rules. Are they restrictive or outdated? Do they communicate distrust or perpetuate excessive bureaucracy? Some rules were written so long ago that employees no longer remember the reason for them. One company we know had a rule against allowing children in the office. Employees all knew the rule and followed it, but no one knew the reason behind it. Finally, someone discovered that when the rule was written, the office held equipment that was dangerous to children, and

For everyone to perform their best, you must lay a foundation of trust and safety.

Monty Roberts believes wholeheartedly in the power of trust and safety. This belief makes those he works with want to do their best, which subsequently puts him at the top of his profession. What makes his case unusual is that Roberts works with horses.

With traditional methods it takes four to six weeks to "break" a wild horse—to tame it enough that it can be saddled and ridden. But Roberts breaks a horse in 25 minutes. How?

As a racehorse breeder and trainer in Solvang, California, Roberts uses alternative methods to break horses. Instead of whipping the horse into submission, he gains its trust by making the horse feel safe. He says he "listens" to the horse and understands it. Because he's broken so many horses, he's able to predict their movements; he knows when an animal will run, when it will slow down and when it can be safely touched. Once Roberts gains the horse's trust, he wins its cooperation. Rather than being a controller, he thinks of the animals as athletes and works with them as a coach would. He's trained some of the world's fastest horses with this unique approach, and believes his horses are so successful because they *want* to race and want to win.

the rule was meant to protect them. Years later, the equipment was long gone, but the rule was still being blindly enforced.

Another organization immersed in outdated rules asked employees to make a list of what they thought were silly or unnecessary regulations. They called this the "Silly Little Rules" list. Inviting employee comments opened the door to greater safety, creativity, and freedom of expression. Encouraging people to search for things that could be improved is the first step toward finding creative solutions.

Yet another company found that many of its best ideas were squelched by management. Why? Management had a rule requiring any new idea to be approved by the employee's immediate supervisor before the company would follow up on it. They changed the rule so that every idea turned down by the supervisors now goes straight to the CEO for consideration. They immediately found they were getting some of their best new ideas that way.

A suggestion box is an old device but it can still spur creative thinking. Some large companies encourage suggestions as a way to come up with cost-cutting techniques. If an employee's idea works, he's rewarded with a percentage of the savings. When it comes to implementing suggestions, however, American companies lag behind their Japanese competitors. Japanese firms implement 95 percent of their employees' suggestions, while American firms implement only 5 percent, reports Joyce Wycoff in *Transformational Thinking*.

At Hawthorne/Stone our policy was to choose a new idea every Monday and try it for a week. Anyone could suggest ways to get things done better, but we all had to agree to give 100 percent commitment to trying the idea, no matter what our personal opinion about it. At the end of the

Openness to creativity brings results in many areas.

The accounting firm of Lipschultz, Levin & Gray was looking for ways to ease individual employee tension, which the firm's chief executive, Steven Siegel, says "dulls the mind." The company also needed to find a way to keep employees from leaving to go work for bigger firms.

The solution Siegel found was anything but usual. When work gets tense, he puts on a gorilla mask. On occasion, a clerk will greet clients while wearing a chicken costume. And when a new client joins the firm, a loud foghorn sounds in the office. Employees can now wear more casual clothes to work and are encouraged to take time during the day to play darts or miniature golf in the office. This approach makes for fun in a business that is often thought of as exceedingly dull.

The firm says its antics actually help business, and they've succeeded in luring business away from some of the biggest accounting firms, which the clients claim are "too stuffy." At Lipschultz, Levin & Gray, clients find they not only get their problems solved, they also feel more at ease. The firm is solving its employee problem, too. Since the new, relaxed attitude was instituted, employee turnover has dropped from eight people a year to only one in the last three-year period. (Adapted from *The Wall Street Journal*, January 18, 1995.)

week, we would decide whether or not to continue implementing the new idea, depending on how successful it was. Everyone was encouraged to share their ideas without fear of criticism, since we were constantly looking for ways to improve our work.

How to Be a Creative Thinker

Creative thinkers and innovators share certain traits. Keep them in mind and apply them as you go through your day and you may find yourself coming up with innovative solutions of your own. Here are the most common traits of creative people:

They Seek What Might Work Better

Creative thinkers don't accept things as they are; instead they look for ways to improve situations. Management consultant Fred Pryor says creativity is " . . . seeing what everyone else sees, but thinking what no one else thinks." In fact, creative thinkers don't see problems, they see challenges—opportunities to stretch their minds in search of innovations. Rather than avoiding troublesome situations, these people face them head-on. They seek out flaws and try to correct them. These are often the little things, pet peeves we take for granted in our everyday lives.

They're Paradigm-Busters

A paradigm is a set of rules or a frame of reference. We use paradigms to define our world and see things more clearly, but they can obscure opportunities and new solutions. For example, some publishing companies still produce their manuscripts without the aid of computers, even though using computers with word processors would be much more efficient. These companies are still doing things the old way, the way it's always been done, and for

Creative thinkers and innovators share certain traits.

Common traits of creative people:

They seek what might work better

::

They're paradigm-busters

::

They develop inquisitive minds

::

They take action

some, using a computer is outside the publishing paradigm. This failure to shift paradigms is costing them time and money.

Anyway, creative thinkers are paradigm-busters: they break through perceived boundaries in their search for solutions. They examine situations from many angles and are able to make dramatic shifts in thinking, called "paradigm shifts," to reach a solution or compromise.

They Develop Inquisitive Minds

For creative thinkers, curiosity is a way of life. They're always asking "why" and wondering how things work. They're fascinated by the world around them, wanting to know how the VCR gets a picture off a tape and onto a screen, how a computer stores information, and what is the actual process for recycling aluminum cans. Knowing how things operate can help us make improvements in the ways we live and work.

Steve Curtis, president of The Marketing Institute, teaches creativity to corporations and at several universities. When asked what would be the one key to unlocking a person's creativity, he replied, "Getting rid of judgment." We limit our ideas by judging them unworthy before we even get them down on paper.

Dr. Yoshio Nakamata is a creative thinker who holds 2,300 patents. His inventions include the floppy disk, compact disk, CD player, digital watch, and water-powered engine. Dr. Nakamata lives by this creed, "Stuff your brain, keep pumping information into it. Give your brain lots of raw material, then give it a chance to cook."

They Take Action

Innovators take creative ideas to fruition: questioning everything, looking at things in different ways, and taking needed action .because they're aware of trends and they test-market and ask questions. They also have the drive to make things happen, by focusing on who they are, what they want, and what it will take to get them where they want to go. Innovators discover the steps necessary to take their idea from the drawing board to reality.

Creative Planning and Problem-Solving

Regardless of whether you consider yourself creative or not, you can use the Creative Planning and Problem-Solving Method, a variation of the Creative Problem-Solving process (CPS), developed by Alex Osborn in 1963. It can help you generate numerous ideas, choose which ones are best, and then take action. It's a three-step process.

1. Understand the Goal or Problem

Whether you're planning for the future or meeting a challenge, you must clearly define your situation and determine what a desirable outcome might be. Clarity is the key to understanding your situation and coming up with the best solution. Define your parameters. What exactly will reaching the goal look like?

Let's say your goal is to learn to juggle. What are the parameters of juggling? You must keep three or more balls in the air at the same time and for several minutes, throwing them up and down in a circular pattern. Once you've clarified the goal (keeping balls in the air), it's easier to come up with a plan of action.

In business, it's rarely this easy to define your goal or challenge. While you're embroiled in a situation, your emotions may run high and cloud your view. Stay calm, think of yourself as someone outside the company or new to the situation, and rid yourself of all assumptions and prejudices. Ask lots of questions—doubt everything, even what seems obviously true. The "obvious" things may be false assumptions. Make sure you look at all sides of the situation.

The fish bone diagram is a useful tool for clarifying problems. Developed by Dr. Kaoru Ishikawa of the University of Tokyo, this chart visually arranges information to make it easier to grasp and process.

To make a fish bone chart, first draw a horizontal line in the center of your paper. (This is the fish's spine.) On the right end of the line, write down the problem. Draw the fish "bones" at 45 degree angles from the horizontal line. Label the bones with appropriate categories, such as "staff," "marketing," or "contracts." You may do this yourself, or create a small team to brainstorm possible causes of the problem in each area and write them along the bones.

Write down everything. Don't judge the information at this point, just throw out ideas. Then, go back over your fish bone and highlight the causes you believe have the most impact and the problem areas you want to address first. Decide on just one problem area and continue the process.

2. Generate Ideas

Creative thinkers generate ideas—lots of ideas. The more ideas they have, the greater their options. They keep up with the latest technology and see others' inventions as a springboard for their own work. They never have a shortage of ideas to work on.

You'll learn how to make your ideas multiply using a process of divergent and convergent thinking. During this process you want to come up with as many ideas and solutions as possible, no matter how unusual or unfeasible they may seem. It's often the outlandish idea that sparks a truly

Making a fish bone diagram helps clarify situations.

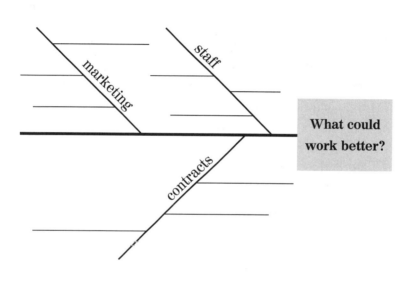

What could work better?

creative solution. The best way to get great ideas is to get lots of ideas.

Divergent Thinking

The process of generating ideas relies on divergent thinking; that is, allowing your thoughts to go in many directions at once. Work with others and encourage everyone to say whatever pops into their head. One idea will lead to another. Write all the ideas down, even if they seem silly at the time.

Remember, anything goes. Forbid criticism and encourage people to blurt out ideas. Divergent thinking comes easiest to the abstract-random learner or the "Squiggle." These learners can easily jump from one idea to the next. The concrete-sequential learners, however, may have trouble switching topics abruptly and putting wild ideas down on paper; they want to finish things and be realistic. (They'll shine later, during planning and action steps.) Try to include as many different types of learners in your group as possible to get a wide range of ideas.

Again, the number-one key to creativity and innovation is to remove judgment. Steve Curtis suggests saying the words, "I wish" before coming up with your next idea. Many times, we stop ourselves from putting ideas on the board because we think they have to be feasible or that we already know the solution. When we say "I wish," we bypass that judgment.

When generating ideas, look to the world around you. Other people—including your competitors—can be your most valuable resources. When I'm considering advertising in a new publication, I call existing advertisers of programs similar to ours. I introduce myself and ask them what kind of results they're getting with their ads. I also ask what other media they advertise in. Surprisingly, these people

Divergent thinking means allowing your thoughts to go in many directions at once.

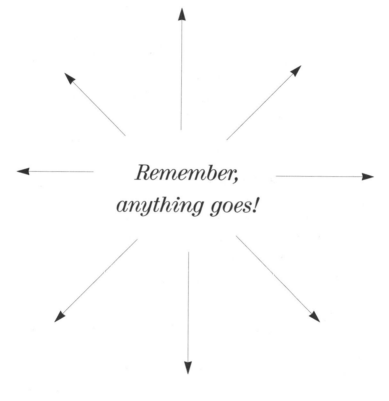

Remember, anything goes!

are almost always willing to talk, and I return the favor by sharing information about my advertising campaign.

I've found we get better results when our ads are grouped with those of other summer youth programs. By working together, we attract additional prospects who may not have noticed a single advertisement. This creates a place for prospective clients to shop for those items. You see it for car dealerships, home sales, and movie listings. Why not for other businesses?

Incubation Period

Now that you've generated ideas, let them incubate. After brainstorming, let the goal or problem sit in the back of your mind for a while. Go for a walk, jog, or do some other repetitive or relaxing activity. If possible, give yourself a whole day to mull it over and, as Dr. Ishikawa suggests, "let it cook overnight." If you have your team together and want to complete the process, give yourself a moment of quiet reflection before you continue.

As you let it all sink in and take the pressure off, you may experience a sudden flash of insight or an "Aha" reaction. Your intuition is hard at work. Even if you don't experience a sudden insight, you'll be able to approach the next step, convergent thinking, with a clearer mind.

Convergent Thinking

Now take another look at all those great ideas you came up with. You may even want to add an idea or two and any insights gained. Then narrow them down to the best few. Which ones are the most attractive, most practical, or most likely to succeed? Highlight, circle, or star your favorite ideas. Next, decide which one or two you choose to implement. Narrowing your focus to a few ideas is called "convergent thinking." It's easiest for the "squares" who

Convergent Thinking:
Review all the great ideas
you've come up with
and narrow them
down to the best few.

Divergent Thinking
Ideas expand outward

←   →

Convergent Thinking
Ideas contract inward

→   ←

like things clearly defined and for the abstract sequential thinkers, who like creating steps and processes. Prioritize your top choices during this process. If the one you decide to implement doesn't work out, quickly return to another.

3. Action

Plan for Action

After you've made your selection of one or a few ideas you plan to implement, write down the steps you'll take. If it's a big project, start with a general overview, then chunk it down into smaller steps to make it more manageable.

Take Action

An ability to take action distinguishes the successful business person from the ones who merely talk about "what could have been." Some people dream up lots of creative ideas, but never carry them out.

To get yourself started, make a timeline on your calendar, marking deadlines for each step. Delegate tasks and assign project teams, if possible. Check your timeline occasionally to make sure you're on schedule.

Evaluate Action

Include in your plan an evaluation step. After implementing your plan for a period of time, step back and ask yourself "Is this working?" Evaluate the effectiveness of your system and identify which parts are working well and which need fine-tuning. Talk to your customers and your staff to get their feedback. Make necessary changes, or maintain your current system if you decide everything is working at optimum levels.

If you find yourself facing major barriers, return to your brainstorming charts and look at your other ideas. You may want to incorporate some of those plans or maybe change

Creative Planning and Problem-Solving Process

Follow these steps:

1 **Understand**
Goal or problem

2 **Generate Ideas**
Divergent Thinking
Incubation
Convergent Thinking

3 **Action**
Plan for action
Take action
Evaluate action

gears completely. Remember, if something is clearly not working, be flexible and willing to stop.

Repeat the evaluation step until you reach your goal. To avoid obstacles along the way, continue to improve your processes. As in the first and second steps, keep an open mind when evaluating your plan. Try to see all sides of the situation. Stay focused on who you are, what you want, and what it will take to get there.

Creativity and the Keys of Excellence

Using the Keys will help you be both creative and innovative. You'll be more motivated to really put yourself into the process if you discover your WIIFM for solving a problem or coming up with a new idea. Commit yourself 100 percent to an idea for a predetermined amount of time, or until it truly proves to be unsuccessful. Stay Flexible. Try new variations of your plan and be willing to stop implementing an idea that isn't working, no matter the time and energy investment you have put into implementing it. Find the value in your failures and acknowledge Failure Leads to Success. Use what you learn from unsuccessful plans when coming up with new ideas. Take Ownership of the results of your idea, negative or positive. Have a This Is It attitude. Keep Your Balance and Live in Integrity throughout the process, making sure your solution is aligned with your values.

Celebrate Your Learning!

! *Why is it important to use your creative abilities?*

Because businesses today face challenges that have never come up before and meeting those challenges will require creative thought, foresight, and innovation.

! *What is one of the first things you need to bring out creativity in people?*

Creative thinking starts with the right environment, one built on trust and safety.

! *What traits do creative thinkers have?*

Creative thinkers:
1. Seek what might work better
2. Are paradigm-busters
3. Develop inquisitive minds
4. Take action

! *What are the steps to creative planning and problem-solving?*

Follow these steps:
1. Understand the goal or problem
2. Generate ideas
3. Plan for action

17

Balance:
The Ultimate Key

 What is balance and why is it the ultimate key?

 What is the family/career challenge and how can you meet it?

 What is the lesson in the pocketful of rocks?

 What is the key to discovering the "gems" among your pocketful of rocks?

Balance. I call it the ultimate key because it's the one that brings everything together. Being in balance means your mind, body, and emotions are in alignment. You make time for all the important areas of your life: work, family, health, friends, and self. Consequently, you function at your most efficient level.

Staying in balance is an ongoing process demanding continual adjustments. Don't expect to achieve balance on a daily basis; sometimes it may be more like a monthly basis. At times, one area of your life may need more attention than others; a crisis may arise at home, or you might have heavy deadlines at work.

I'm currently putting in 12 hours a day at the office because several important projects are going to get wrapped up over the next few months. I choose to focus on these projects right now because they mean something to me and I want them to succeed. I also know I won't have to put in long hours forever. Once I finish these projects, I can return to a less intense schedule. I may not be getting to the gym as much as I'd like right now, or seeing the latest movies as they come out, but the choice is mine, and I'm aware of making that choice.

Staying in balance takes vigilance. You may need to check in with yourself daily and ask yourself, "What do I value? What's really important to me?" Seemingly conflicting things come up every day that need to be weighed. But if you're honest with yourself and acknowledge that you're making a choice, you'll find it easier to maintain your balance. There's nothing wrong with a man choosing to work 60-hour weeks year after year so as to provide his family with a fancy lifestyle. But he needs to be aware that he's making that choice. And he might want to check with his wife and kids and see if that's a choice they too want him to make. He may be surprised to learn that they would prefer to have fewer possessions if it meant having him around more hours each week.

The Family/Career Challenge

The hypothetical father mentioned above is facing one of the biggest challenges business people confront today: balancing family and career. In 1992, 55 percent of women with a child under age three were working. With so many mothers working, many men are taking a greater role in parenting and doing household chores. Meeting the demands of family and work is challenging for both men and women; a sick child or a late night at the office can quickly throw your life out of balance.

At my company, many employees have young children. Each employee has found different ways to balance work and family time. Some opt to work part-time; others start work early so they can be home by mid-afternoon when their children return from school. We support our employees by sanctioning flex-time and by allowing them to work part-time whenever possible. One of our employees works at home a few days a week, telecommuting via phone and computer modem. Life always presents challenges, but with the support of employers, parents are finding creative ways to balance career and family.

As you juggle your time between work and home, remember it's also important to take time for yourself. We all function best when our minds, bodies, and emotions are in balance. Spend as much time as you can taking care of each area. Few of us have as much time as we'd like to take care of each area—so, weigh your priorities, and try to stay in integrity with them. When you have extra demands to meet, your stress level may rise and you may feel as if you can't take time for yourself. But do it anyway. Why? Because it's been proven that taking personal time actually reduces stress. So when the pressure is on, take some time for yourself, even if it's only a few minutes out of the day. Use your Quantum Learning skills to work more efficiently, thereby freeing up time for yourself and your family—making everyone happier and reducing your stress in the process.

Every moment of the day, we're evaluating priorities—deciding what's most important to us in that moment. As I mentioned, I often consciously choose to spend long, focused hours at work. But there are also times when I'll leave work in an instant to attend a family event. When my twin granddaughters were born, I hopped a flight to Chicago the next day to welcome them into the world. When friends invited Joe and me to share their villa in Mexico, we jumped at the chance—even though it meant leaving the office for a few days during a busy period. I work hard, so I seize opportunities to play, enjoy family, or spend time by myself whenever I feel I can leave the office. These times are infrequent right now, but that's how I'm choosing to live at this time. It's what I want to do. I feel I'm in control of the situation; it doesn't control me.

When time is at a premium, careful planning can help you make the most of it. Book time for hobbies, family, exercise, and other areas on a time management system or calendar. Stephen Covey has designed a wonderful system for staying in balance. He recommends that each week, you identify the roles you want to play, such as parent, spouse, manager, project coordinator, church member, neighbor—whatever you want to spend time on. Then, decide what goals you want to achieve that week in each area. On your calendar, schedule time to meet those goals. If your goal is to get into shape, you might schedule four nights a week at the gym. If you know you have a presentation to give on Friday, cut your workouts to three evenings and schedule time to practice. You can apply this format to any calendar, or contact the Covey Leadership Center in Provo, Utah about purchasing one of theirs. The roles you play—that is, areas that are important to you—may change from week to week, and that's okay. What's important is keeping your focus on the things that are most important in your life, and making time for them. Then you're in balance; you're living in integrity.

At the office, strive for balance in the workday. There are a number of ways you can do this. If you're working intensely on a project, take short breaks periodically. Give yourself a chance to get up, stretch, walk around, and get a drink of water. Give your brain a moment to rest. This is often the time when the problem you've been pondering for hours suddenly becomes clear. When you break your focus from time to time, you empty your mind—and that leaves a space for a new idea or insight to come in.

If possible, try not to schedule a marathon of meetings. Alternate meeting times with other work: phone calls, projects, and so on.

No matter how busy you are, try to take time for lunch. Your mind and body need energy to work at optimum levels. If you have a long lunch break, work out at a gym, or at least take a walk around the block. Enjoy a change of scenery when possible. Try eating at a nearby restaurant or park. Even a 15-minute snack in the lunchroom can revitalize you, and you'll work more efficiently afterward.

We talked earlier about how, at our company, we try to keep work relationships in balance by making time for celebrations—birthdays, showers, holiday parties, and our annual Vision Meeting. I believe it's important to take time to recognize the milestones in one another's life, and it also builds cohesiveness within the company. Take time to let others know how much you appreciate them.

A Last Look at the 8 Keys

In addition to being the last of the 8 Keys, balance is also the sum of all the others. Let's look at them again briefly.

1. Live in Integrity

    Balance and integrity go hand-in-hand. If your values and behavior aren't aligned, it's almost impossible to keep your mind, body, and spirit in alignment.

2. Acknowledge that Failure Leads to Success

    Being in balance is all about learning from our mistakes, and doing what it takes to get back in balance.

3. Speak with Good Purpose

    Be honest and direct, and speak in a positive sense. It's easier to maintain balance if you're honest with friends, family, and colleagues about the demands on your time, and what you can and can't do.

4. Live in the Now—This Is It!

    Develop the ability to focus your attention on the present moment. Each moment, each task counts. Living in the now is what gives our lives balance.

5. Affirm Your Commitment

    As you strive for balance, make sure what you're doing now aligns with your vision of the future. Be committed to your vision, and the time you spend will become more valuable and worthwhile.

It's important to take time to recognize the milestones in one another's life.

Let others know how much you appreciate them.

6. Take Ownership

Be accountable and responsible. Stephen Covey's system for staying in balance depends on you taking ownership of your various roles—spouse, manager, project coordinator, etc.—and then following through with the responsibilities of those roles.

7. Stay Flexible

Maintain the ability to change what you're doing to get the outcome you desire. For example, flexibility is essential for those facing the family/career challenge.

8. Keep Your Balance

Use all of the previous keys to maintain your mind, body, and spirit in alignment.

Integrate Your Learning, Balance Your Life

As you go about the daily business of living, you have the opportunity to gather things that can be valuable to you. Let me explain what I mean through a story, told to me by learning consultant, John LeTellier.

A man was walking from one part of the country to another. Since dawn, he'd been traveling over unfamiliar land . . . the sun high and hot over his head. As the day wore on, a strange feeling came over him; he realized he'd been walking all day without seeing another traveler. He began to think he must be on the wrong road.

As it grew later, he became more concerned. Retracing the journey in his mind, he strove to see if he had taken a wrong turn. Suddenly, he thought he saw something out of the corner of his eye. Turning around, he stepped back in surprise. There at the side of the road was a very old man sitting so still and limp the traveler almost mistook him for

Balance is the sum of all of the 8 Keys.

Live in Integrity

Conduct yourself in the state of authenticity, sincerity, and wholeness that results when your values and behavior are aligned.

Acknowledge that Failure Leads to Success

Understand failures simply provide us with the information we need to learn so we can succeed.

Speak with Good Purpose

Develop the skill of speaking in a positive sense, being responsible for honest and direct communication.

Live in the Now—This Is It!

Develop the ability to focus your attention on the present moment. Each moment, each task counts.

Affirm Your Commitment

Follow your vision without wavering; stay true to the course. Do whatever it takes to get the job done.

Take Ownership

Be accountable and responsible. Be someone who can be counted upon, someone who responds.

Stay Flexible

Maintain the ability to change what you are doing to get the outcome you desire.

Keep Your Balance

Maintain your mind, body, and spirit in alignment.

a rock. The old man's head hung down and his shoulders hunched forward. A thick mane of silvery hair hid his face.

The traveler stared, unsure what to do. Then, he called out, "Excuse me, sir, are you all right?" The old man didn't answer.

"I wonder," said the traveler, "could you tell me if I'm on the right road." Still no response.

"Excuse me, excuse me, sir, are you all right?" he asked again, but the old man sat perfectly still. The traveler gently touched the man's arm, and asked again if he was okay. But there was no response.

"I don't know what to do with this old man," he said to himself. "I'll have to find someone and tell them he's here." Suddenly, the old man lifted his head and stared deep into the traveler's eyes. The traveler said, "Can you hear me? I haven't seen another soul all day, and I don't know if I'm on the right road."

Finally, very slowly, the old man's ancient voice creaked out a response, "When you get to the river, gather up what you find before you cross." Then he slumped back down and wouldn't say another word.

The traveler thought, "That's it? That's the end of the conversation? He's got to be crazy. I must be on my way."

But then he wondered, "What did he mean, 'When you get to the river, gather up what you find before you cross'? There probably isn't even a river."

The traveler moved on, and as he rounded a bend, there before him lay a beautiful winding river. As he stepped into the water, the old man's words came back to him: "When you get to the river, gather up what you find before you cross." The traveler glanced around him, but all he saw were some rocks, so he reached back, grabbed a handful and stuffed them into his pocket. The rocks were heavy

And the old man said . . .

*"When you get to the river, gather up what
you find before you cross."*

and cumbersome, and halfway across the river he thought, "Why am I doing this? I should just drop these useless rocks and be on my way." But instead he carried them all to the other side and continued on down the path.

At sunset he stopped to rest. As he lay down, the rocks, which were still in his pocket, made him uncomfortable. So he reached in and pulled them out, intending to throw them away. But before he did, he noticed how brightly they glowed in the evening light. Taking a closer look, he realized that the rocks had been miraculously transformed into beautiful gemstones. The man was astonished, and said to himself, "If only I had gathered more stones before I crossed the river."

Life is truly a journey. Along the way, you'll meet people, travel different places, and feel a variety of emotions. Many of these things may seem mundane, routine, and meaningless. But as you gather up life's experiences, be alert. You never know what may turn out to be a gem. Some of the most precious gems you'll find along the way may be those things you learn that seem unimportant at the time. When you learn something new, it usually connects to something you've learned in the past. It can also be integrated with something you'll learn in the future.

Look at learning as a continuous process. Each new thing you learn is a building block, a step toward greater knowledge. As you build up your base of knowledge and skill, you climb toward greater success. So the more you know, the better. Knowledge from seemingly unrelated areas can actually enhance your own area of expertise, if you learn how to apply it. Taking a broader view of your career, for example, can help you recognize how to apply all your skills.

College students often complain about the many courses

And the traveler said . . .

*"If only I had gathered more stones before
I crossed the river."*

they're required to take that aren't related to their degree. For engineering students, English feels like a rock dragging them down. But studies show that engineers in supervisory positions spend 80 percent of their time communicating, and only 20 percent of their time working on engineering. Engineers with good writing skills make more money. Thus, for an engineer, the rock called "English" becomes a gemstone.

Learning also carries over in more subtle ways. You probably studied science in school, and unless you're a scientist, you may never have used scientific formulas in your career. But you probably do some problem-solving, and knowing how to explore and experiment helps you to come up with solutions. Likewise, it's unlikely you've been asked to recite Shakespeare in a job interview. But the writing and analytical thinking skills you learned in English class are valuable in nearly any profession. All knowledge is a resource that can be applied in some form. Recognize these hidden gems in your own experience and discover how they fit into your career.

As technology changes, so do our jobs. Many jobs have actually become obsolete. More and more people are finding they need to change fields to survive—sometimes after spending 25 or 30 years in a specialized position. Often, these people feel their experience doesn't count for anything in their new jobs. But they're mistaken. Experience is a valuable asset—if you know how present it.

Many of the skills you learn in one profession can be carried over to new careers. I know of a man who had several seemingly unrelated careers: teacher, advertising salesman, lawyer, stockbroker. For a while he was reluctant to show anyone his resumé, because it looked as if he was bouncing around not knowing what to do with his life.

But he loved to write and eventually became a financial writer. When he did, he was able to draw upon what he'd learned in all his previous professions and do a better job for his clients than if he'd had experience in just one or two fields. The abandoned professions, which looked like rocks weighing down his resumé, turned out to be gemstones in the end.

Discovering Your Gems

The key to discovering gems among your pocketful of rocks is exploration. You have a lifetime of skills, knowledge, and experiences to draw on that are uniquely your own. Recognize the valuable gifts you have to offer, as Buckminster Fuller did when he considered ending his own life, " . . . I realized that each of us is an incredible inventory of experiences, and that I might be able to use some of my experiences . . . so that I could help others from coming to the same pains I had come to." (From *Fuller's Earth,* by Richard J. Brenneman, St. Martin's Press, New York, 1984.)

Take a look at the knowledge you've gained just by reading this book. You've learned:

- How to find your own intrinsic motivation.
  (This Is It!)

- The power of taking responsibility for your life.
  (Ownership)

- How to identify your preferred learning style.
  (Psycho-Geometrics, Gregorc, VAK)

- How to take meaningful notes.
  (Mind Mapping, Mindscaping, and Notes:TM)

- How to read faster with greater comprehension.
  (Quantum Reading)

- The benefit of turning failure into feedback. (Failure Leads to Success)

- How to memorize anything: names, numbers, and lists. (Peg system, association)

- Creative thinking and problem-solving. (3 steps for creative planning and problem-solving)

- The power of clear communication. (Speak with Good Purpose; Four-Part Apology)

These are your gems. Take a few moments to think about how you can use each of them in your life. Be open to new applications. Exploring takes imagination, seeing old problems with "new eyes." Once you have a clear picture of how you'll apply your skills, make time to practice them on specific tasks. The only way these skills will work for you is through practice and review. At first, using them may seem awkward, but eventually it will become second nature. The only way to make this happen, though, is with conscious effort and practice.

Commit yourself to practicing your skills. Think of specific ways you can apply Quantum Learning and the 8 Keys in your life, and write them down. For example: Use speed-reading skills to read the newspaper in the evening. Speak with Good Purpose during marketing meetings. Review them periodically and keep practicing; soon these skills will become a habit.

As you look for more gems in your life, keep an open mind. Turn problems into opportunities. Instead of seeing roadblocks, see interesting detours to explore the countryside. Instead of fearing a potential layoff as impending doom, view it as an opportunity to find a more fulfilling career, to spend time with family, or to go back to school.

Take a look at the knowledge you've gained just by reading this book.

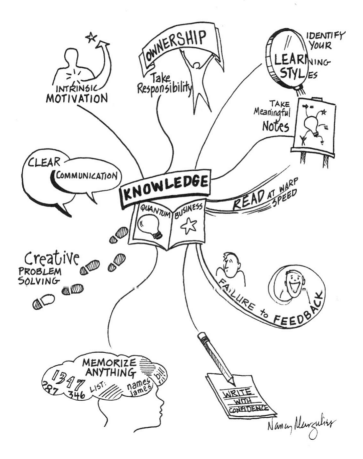

In life, you find what you're looking for. If you expect a series of failed job interviews, that's what you'll end up with. But if you expect to find a job that fits your needs, you'll probably find one. Clarify what you want and hold that picture in your mind. Write it down, and read what you've written—regularly and often.

When you explore your options, let your imagination run wild. The wildest ideas may be the ones that spark the solution. Even dreams may hold the answer. The structure of DNA was discovered when the pieces of the puzzle came together in a dream. Brainstorm, then Mind Map your ideas to further organize and develop them.

The more you explore, the more options you'll have. With more options available, more rocks can be transformed into gemstones, and the more success you'll have in business and in life.

Celebrate Your Learning!

! *What is balance and why is it the ultimate key?*

Balance means your mind, body, and emotions are in alignment. It's the ultimate key because it brings everything else together.

! *What is the family/career challenge, and how can you meet it?*

With so many women working these days, people have more demands to balance their work and family lives. Some ways to do it:

1. Ask for flex-time or part-time work.
2. Give priority to what's important to you.
3. Plan carefully.
4. Take breaks.
5. Celebrate.

! *What is the lesson in the pocketful of rocks?*

As you go through life, you have many opportunities to gather things that can be of value to you. Rather than immediately rejecting them, keep them—you don't know what may have real value later on.

! *What is the key to discovering the "gems" among your pocketful of rocks?*

Exploration. Look at your life; note all the experience and knowledge you've gained. These are your "gems."

Congratulations!

You've learned ways to:

Strengthen the foundation and culture of your company

::

Create an empowering environment

::

Foster positive relationships

::

Increase your motivation

::

Stretch your mind

::

Rediscover the joy of learning

*Practice your Quantum Learning skills,
live the 8 Keys, and
celebrate your new success!*

Permissions

Mind Mapping® is a registered trademark of Buzan Organizations. Used with permission from Tony Buzan, Harleyford Manor Estate, Marlow, Buckinghamshire, SL7 2DX, England.

The Fuller Projection Dymaxion™ Map is a registred trademark. Used with permission from the Buckminster Fuller Institute, 2040 Alameda Padre Sierra, #224, Santa Barbara, CA 93103.

Excerpt from *Rolling Thunder* by Doug Boyd. Copyright 1974 by Doug Boyd. Reprinted by permission from Random House, Inc. 201 East 50th Street, New York, NY 10103.

Excerpts from *Psycho-Geometrics, How to Use Geometric Psychology to Influence People,* by Susan Dellinger, Ph.D. Copyright 1989 by Prentice-Hall, Inc., Englewood Cliffs, NJ 07632

Excerpts from *How Your Child Is Smart,* by Dawna Markova. Copyright 1992 by Dawna Markova. Reprinted by permission from Conari Press, 2550 Ninth Street, Ste. 101, Berkeley, CA 94710.

"The Einstein Factor" by Win Wenger and Richard Poe. Reprinted in part with permission from Success Magazine, 230 Park Avenue, New York, NY 10169.

Excerpts of *Principle-Centered Leadership* and *7 Habits of Highly Effective People* by Stephen R. Covey used with permission of Covey Leadership Center, Inc. 3507 North University Avenue, Ste. 100, Provo, UT 84604-4479. (800) 331-7716.

Recommended Reading

Blanchard, Ken. *Raving Fans.* Melbourne, Australia:
The Business Library, 1993.

Boyd, Doug. *Rolling Thunder.* New York: Random House,
1974.

Buzan, Tony. *The Mind Map Book.* New York: Dutton, 1994.

Buzan, Tony. *Use Your Perfect Memory.* New York: Penguin
Books, 1991.

Byham, William. *Zapp!.* New York: Fawcett, 1992.

Canfield, Jack and Mark Victor Hansen. *Chicken Soup for the
Soul.* Deerfield Beach, Florida: Health Communications Inc.,
1993.

Covey, Stephen R. *Principle-Centered Leadership.* New York:
Summit Books, 1991.

Covey, Stephen R. *The 7 Habits of Highly Effective People.*
New York: Simon & Schuster, 1989.

Damasio, Antonio R. *Descartes' Error.* New York: Putnam,
1994.

Dellinger, Susan. *Psycho-Geometrics, How to Use Geometric
Psychology to Influence People.* Englewood Cliffs, NJ:
Prentice-Hall, 1989.

DePorter, Bobbi. *Quantum Learning: Unleashing the Genius in You.* New York: Dell Publishing, 1992.

Dunn, Dunn, and Price. *Learning Styles Inventory Manual.* Learning Styles Center, St. Johns University, 8000 Utopia Parkway, Jamaica, NY, 11439. (718) 990-6335.

Geier, John, G. *Personal Profile System.* Performax Systems International. 1415 Whyte Avenue, Winnipeg, Manitoba, R3E 1V7. Canada. (800) 665-7535 or (204) 772-3728. 1979.

Gregorc, Antony. *An Adult's Guide to Style.* Maynard, MA: Gabriel System, 1982.

Hernacki, Mike. *The Ultimate Secret to Getting Absolutely Everything You Want.* New York: Berkley Books, 1988.

Herrmann, Ned. *The Creative Brain.* Lake Lure, NC: Brain Books, 1988.

Higgins, James. *101 Problem-Solving Techniques.* Winter Park, FL: New Management, 1994.

Huang, Chungliang Al and Lynch, Jerry. *Mentoring, The Tao of Giving and Receiving Wisdom.* San Francisco, CA: HarperSanFrancisco, 1995.

Jensen, Eric. *The Learning Brain.* San Diego, CA: Turning Point Publishing, 1995.

Land, George. *Break Point and Beyond.* New York: Harper Business, 1992.

Margulies, Nancy. *Mapping Inner Space.* Tuscon: Zephyr Press, 1991.

Markova, Dawna. *How Your Child Is Smart*. Berkeley, CA: Conari Press, 1992.

Parker, Glenn, M. *Team Players and Teamwork*. San Francisco: Jossey-Bass, Inc., 1990.

Senge, Peter. *The Fifth Discipline: The Art and Practice of the Learning Organization*. New York: Doubleday, 1994.

Snyder, Robert. *BUCKMINSTER FULLER: An Autobiographical Monologue/Scenario*. New York: St. Martin's Press, 1980. Available through Buckminster Fuller Institute, (805) 962-0022.

Wenger, Win and Richard Poe. *The Einstein Factor*. Rocklin, CA: Prima Publishing, 1995.

Wycoff, Joyce. *Mindmapping, Your Personal Guide to Exploring Creativity and Problem Solving*. New York: Berkley Books, 1991.

Wycoff, Joyce. *Transformational Thinking*. New York: Berkley Books, 1995.

Organizations and Resources

Blanchard Training and Development
125 State Place
Escondido, CA 92025

Buckminster Fuller Institute
2040 Alameda Padre Sierra, #224
Santa Barbara, CA 93103

Buzan Centres
In the United States:
415 Federal Highway
Lake Park, FL 33403

In the United Kingdom:
Harleyford Manor Estate
Marlow
Buckinghamshire, SL7 2DX
England

Covey Leadership Center
3507 North University Avenue, Ste. 100
Provo, UT 84604

Educational Discoveries
The Accounting Game
5495 Arapahoe Rd., Ste. 205
Boulder, CO 80303

Global Energy Network International (GENI)
P.O. Box 81565
San Diego, CA 92138

Innovation Network
34 East Sola Street
Santa Barbara, CA 93101

International Alliance for Learning
1040 First Street
Encinitas, CA 92024

Learning Forum
SuperCamp
Quantum Learning Programs
1725 South Coast Highway
Oceanside, CA 92054

Learning Strategies Corporation
PhotoReading
900 East Wayzata Boulevard
Wayzata, MN 55391

Meta Quality
P.O. Box 102
Old Greenwich, CT 06870

The Tahoe Group
The Awareness Game
P.O. Box 4268
Incline Village, NV 89450

Index

Scheele, Paul, 200
7 Habits of Highly Effective People, 70
Skills
creativity as, 318–319
in Quantum Reading, 204–298
retooling, 4–8
training
SuperCamp approach, 23
Snyder, Steve, 190
Soft focus, 206
Special Theory of Relativity, 194
Squire, Larry, 88, 238
Success 197
Suggestology, 30
SuperCamp
and Burklyn Business School, 18–20
learning environment at, 22
mental attitude at, importance, 22–23
skill training, 23
SuperScan, 210–213
Sylwester, Robert, 238–239

The Tahoe Group, 179
The Team Player Survey, 136
Technology, changing, 2–3
Thermometer, 277–278
Thermostat, 277–278
Thinkers, types, 122–125
Thinking
convergent, 334–335
creatively, 326–329
divergent, 332–333
patterns, 128–132
changing, 226–227
Thurber, Marshall, 8–9, 65
TM, *See* Notes:TM
Transformational Thinking, 318, 324
Traveler's story, 348–352
Tri-Focus, 206–207
Triune brain, 86
Turner, Ted, 146

Use Your Perfect Memory, 284

Values
and behavior, 98
discovering, 101
Visible communication, 71–73
Vision
committing to, 274–277
discovering, 272
Vision Meetings, 52–56
agenda, 55
Vos-Groenendal, Dr. Jeannette, 23

Wagner, Peter, 13
Wenger, Win, 166
What's In It For Me, 86, 92–94
commitment and, 274–275
memory improvement and, 238–239
What You Think of Me Is None of My Business, 226
WIIFM, *See* What's In It For Me
Wilde, Oscar, 229
"The Wizard of Oz," 249
Wycoff, Joyce, 160, 318, 324

Zyman, Sergio, 230